CASE STUDIES IN
EDUCATION AND CULTURE

General Editors

GEORGE *and* LOUISE SPINDLER
Stanford University

NICHŪ

A Japanese School

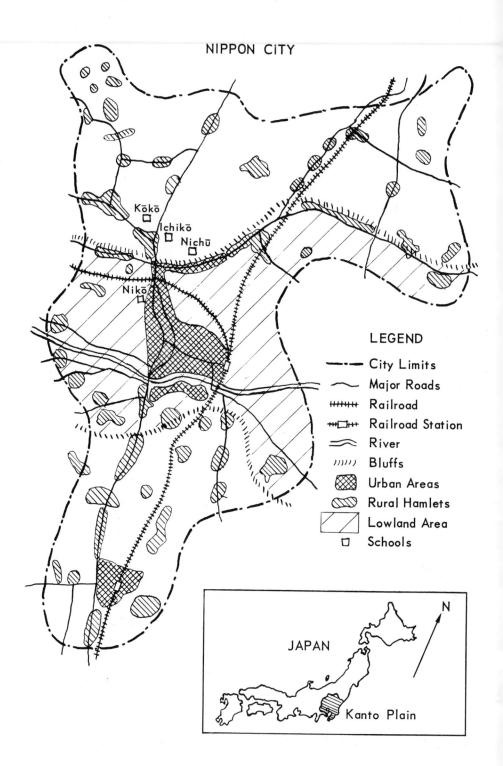

NIPPON CITY

Kōkō
Ichikō
Nichū
Nikō

LEGEND

—··—	City Limits
⌒	Major Roads
⊬⊬⊬⊬	Railroad
⊬⊡⊬	Railroad Station
⌇⌇	River
)))))	Bluffs
▨	Urban Areas
▨	Rural Hamlets
▨	Lowland Area
⊡	Schools

JAPAN

N

Kanto Plain

NICHŪ
A Japanese School

JOHN SINGLETON
University of Pittsburgh

HOLT, RINEHART AND WINSTON

New York • *Chicago* • *San Francisco* • *Toronto* • *London*

To my research associates
        Peter, William, Mark, and Anne.

Foreword

About the Series

This series of case studies in education and culture is designed to bring to students in professional education and in the social sciences the results of direct observation and participation in educational process in a variety of cultural settings. Individual studies will include some devoted to single classrooms, others will focus on single schools, some on large communities and their schools; still others will report on indigenous cultural transmission where there are no schools at all in the Western sense. Every attempt will be made to move beyond the formalistic treatments of educational process to the interaction between the people engaged in educative events, their thinking and feeling, and the content of the educational process in which they are engaged. Each study will be basically descriptive in character but since all of them are about education they are also problem-oriented. Interpretive generalizations are produced inductively. Some are stated explicitly by the authors of the studies. Others are generated in the reader's mind as hypotheses about education and its environmental relationships.

The cross-cultural emphasis of the series is particularly significant. Education is a cultural process. Each new member of a society or a group must learn to act appropriately as a member and contribute to its maintenance and, occasionally, to its improvement. Education, in every cultural setting, is an instrument for survival. It is also an instrument for adaptation and change. To understand education we must study it as it is—imbedded in the culture of which it is an integral part and which it serves.

When education is studied this way, the generalizations about the relationship between schools and communities, educational and social systems, education and cultural setting that are current in modern educational discussions, become meaningful. This series is, therefore, intended for use in courses in comparative and overseas education, social foundations and the sociology of education, international educational development, culture and personality, social psychology, cultural dynamics and cultural transmission, comparative sociology—wherever the interdependency of education and culture, and education and society, is particularly relevant.

We hope these studies will be useful as resources for comparative analyses, and for stimulating thinking and discussion about education that is not confined by one's own cultural experience. Without this exercise of a comparative, transcultural perspective it seems unlikely that we can acquire a clear view of our own educational experience, or view education in other cultural settings without ethnocentric bias.

About the Author

John Singleton is an associate professor in the International and Development Education Program of the University of Pittsburgh. He spent eighteen months in Japan during 1961–1963 studying the Japanese language and carrying out the field-work for his doctoral dissertation at Stanford University's International Development Education Center. Before his doctoral studies, he worked with elementary school teachers as an education and training specialist in the Truk District of the U.S. Trust Territory of the Pacific Islands. While carrying out his field research in Japan, his introduction to the rural hamlet where he and his family established residence was facilitated by a local shopkeeper who had lived on Truk before World War II. Other related experiences have included work and research on the Papago Indian Reservation, the North Carolina Cherokee Indian Reservation, two years as a high school teacher at the Fort Totten Indian School in North Dakota, and three years as Associate Director of the International Development Fellowships and Seminars Programs of the East-West Center at the University of Hawaii. He is a fellow of the Society for Applied Anthropology.

About the Book

This case study in education and culture centers upon a single school near an urban center of population in Japan. Its special strength lies in the close scrutiny of the structure and process of education within this single school and its immediate environment. The organization of the classroom, examination procedures, parental attitudes towards the school and schooling, the operation of the PTA and various other councils within the community, the interaction of school administrators and teachers, the teachers and their roles, and the interaction of teachers and the teachers' union are all carefully described. The level of description is ethnographic. Specific incidents, people, and situations are described within a framework of more formal generalization and interpretation. The patterning of activities and sentiments is clear but the direct observation and reporting of behavior never permits the reader to wander off into abstractions or leaves him with form but little content. This level of descriptive analysis is lacking to a surprising degree in the existing literature, and, in our opinion, is badly needed. But Dr. Singleton does not let his case rest with the ethnographic description of this single school and its locale. The larger context of education in Japan is also considered. He gives us an understanding of the national political and educational issues that influence education at the local level. The result is a complex and satisfying treatment of education in a culture enough like the West to be understandable and different enough to be interesting.

George and Louise Spindler
General Editors
STANFORD, 1966

Acknowledgments

The first requirement for a cross-cultural "rice roots" study of Japanese education is a school and community willing to accept a foreign researcher intruding in the areas of life and activity to which he would not normally be invited as observer or participant. The people of the community that I shall call Nippon City and the staff of the Nichū Middle School showed both patience and understanding in their acceptance of myself and my family as foreign students of Japan, as neighbors, and as friends. Because this book records many highly personal details, the real names of the community, its school, and its inhabitants have been changed for the sake of annonymity. The first acknowledgment must be made collectively, therefore, to these citizens of Nippon City who made the ten-month period of field research and residence in 1962–1963 not only productive but thoroughly enjoyable.

Each member of my family made a direct contribution to this study. My wife, Anne, patiently maintained the family home while observing and participating in the life of a rural Japanese hamlet. Important research assistants in their father's enterprise were my three sons. Mark entered the first grade of the rural elementary school, allowing us to experience, as well as to observe, the role of parents in the Japanese school system. William, likewise, introduced us to the delightful world of the Japanese kindergarten. Peter, born one month before we moved to Nippon City, provided a very special insight into Japanese child care as we watched the reactions of friends and neighbors to our American patterns of child care. Because our children were there, our neighbors had the satisfaction of conducting their own counter-study of comparative Japanese and American family relations.

The fieldwork for this study was originally reported in my doctoral dissertation for the School of Education at Stanford University. My three major advisers there have contributed importantly to the analysis of my field data. Professor Paul R. Hanna, Director of the Stanford International Development Education Center, stimulated my interest in studying education as an instrument of national policy in Japan and then made many of the arrangements for my fieldwork. Professor George Spindler of the Stanford Anthropology Department provided the background for the research methodology selected. Professor Kurt Steiner of the Stanford Political Science Department helped with the analysis of Japanese political institutions.

Other people who made significant contributions to the success of the fieldwork and later analysis were Professors Tokiomi Kaigo (now retired), Morihiko Okatsu, and Seiichi Miyahara of the Tokyo University Faculty of Education; Messrs. Yasuo Matsuno and Eiichi Suzuki, then graduate students at Tokyo University; Professor L. Keith Brown of the Anthropology Department, University of Pittsburgh; and Mr. Ryoji Ito and his colleagues in the Research Section, Research Bureau, Ministry of Education, Japan.

For two years of generous financial and moral support, I am grateful to the Ford Foundation and the Foreign Area Fellowship Program. Of course, the conclusions, mistakes, opinions, and other statements in this publication are my own and are not necessarily those of the Ford Foundation or the people named above.

J.S.

Pittsburgh, Pa.
December 1966

Contents

NICHŪ

A Japanese School

Introduction

THIS IS A STUDY of one public school in a Japanese community and the interaction of that school and its personnel with significant groups and forces operating in the broader framework of Japanese national life. The Nichū Middle School provides the last three of nine years of compulsory formal education to all children between the ages of twelve and fifteen living in its district. More than 800 children come to class six days a week from homes in isolated mountain settlements, rural agricultural hamlets, and an urban shopkeeper's neighborhood.

My family and I moved into the Nichū school district and became participant observers of the school and community scene. Observations were made while sitting in the back of a social studies class, attending a teachers union meeting, drinking *sake* at the mayor's home on New Year's Day, and participating in the everyday life of the school and its local community. Systematic interview surveys of pupils' families, teachers, and PTA officials supplemented the data gained from participant observation.

In a study of a school and community, the conception one has of the school as a social institution will affect the type of data collected as well as its analysis. A model proposed by Bernard Siegel (1955) for the study of American school systems suggested the basic organization for the present study. Viewing the school, itself, as an educational community in contact with other specific groups, communities, or organizations, one can describe each of these important entities and its relations with the school. Most important to an understanding of the school's role in society are the consequences of the interaction of the school with the forces emanating from the school's socio-political and cultural environment.

In this study of Nichū, three major forces are viewed and described in their interaction with the school, and in the following order:

1. the local community of the school district;
2. the administrative hierarchy of formal education from the local school board to the Ministry of Education;
3. the professional community of Japanese teachers represented primarily by the Japan Teachers Union and its local chapters.

Within the framework of the interrelationships between the school and these forces, a consistent focus is provided for the case study by attention to the goals of education—the perceptions of them in various sectors, and their implementation.

Many of the observations subsumed in this study are related to national political and educational issues. Education in every modern society is in some degree an instrument of national policy, and, in most, a subject of national controversy. This is clearly evident in Japan. Prime ministers have raised the question of national educational goals in openly political speeches. Educational policy has been an explicit issue in election campaigns. Long known for a centrally directed, unified, modern school system, Japan has experienced both constructive and devastating effects from educational programs organized for specified national purposes. Much of the recent controversy has been focused on the two major organizations in education: the Ministry of Education and the Japan Teachers Union.

The Ministry of Education is formally responsible for national interests in education. It is the top level of an administrative chain of command that reaches down to the schools through intervening prefectural and local boards of education.

The Japan Teachers Union (JTU) represents 90 percent of the public elementary and middle school teachers of Japan. It is a focus of opposition to the policies of the government and the Ministry of Education. As a national organization, it supports the Socialist party in Japan. It has a history of "leftist and even Communist-affiliated" leadership (Kawai 1960:200). However, an agreement reached in 1961 withdrew JTU political support from the Communist party.

Antithetical views on educational issues held by the Ministry of Education and the JTU bear a direct relation to their political affiliations. The Ministry of Education is led by the minister of education, one of the members of the Prime Minister's cabinet. With only one short interruption in the postwar period, conservative politicians, now united in the Liberal-Democratic party, have held effective control of the government and, hence, of the Ministry of Education. Within Japan, the Liberal-Democratic party depends on conservative rural areas for voting support, but is primarily the political representative of business interests. The Socialist party is the party of organized labor and depends on urban voters for support.

When new educational policies have been initiated by the ministry, they have been consistently opposed by the JTU and the Socialist party. Often, ministry policy has been a direct threat to the JTU. There has been little direct communication between the ministry and the JTU.

Specific Ministry of Education policies have been viewed by the JTU as attempts by the ministry to strengthen its control over local schools and teachers. Though many arguments have been given against each innovation of the ministry, the fear that it is intending to destroy the union and the democratic innovations of the postwar American Occupation seems to be the important explanation of the JTU stand.

The underlying issue in this controversy is the JTU view that the Government and the Ministry are seeking to revive militaristic national patterns of behavior from the prewar period. Each move of the government and Ministry of Education is seen as a return to the past, a past from which the JTU and a large group of Japanese intellectuals want to disassociate themselves.

Reconciliation with Japan's past or rejection of it, particularly the events and traditions that led up to World War II, is, perhaps, the basic issue that politically divides conservatives and liberals in Japan today.

It is important to take these conditions into account as we attempt to gain an understanding of Nichū Middle School, its interaction with significant groups in its local environment, and the perception and implementation of educational goals within the framework of this interaction. No single school or local community in a complex national society can be treated as though it were an isolable unit. This is particularly true in Japan, due to the conditions summarized above.

The study proceeds in a series of steps, beginning with the Nippon City environment in which the local school system operates. With this environment established, the study then turns to the more immediate local community of Nichū Middle School, to the school itself, and to the interaction between the school and significant groups and forces in this local environment. In these stages of discussion, and in those following, there is constant attention to the varying perceptions of educational goals held by different groups and organizations and the conflicts encountered in their implementation.

The study then shifts to a wider arena. Attention is given to the interaction of the Nichū Middle School with the administrative hierarchy of education in Japan, and between the school and the teachers union. The study ends with an analysis of the sentiments and behaviors of teachers in Nichū School as they cope with the conflicts that constitute such a significant and enduring part of their environment.

The first chapter describes the local community setting of this study, which includes both the wider community of Nippon City and the more localized Nichū school district within the city.

1 / Nippon City and Nichū District

NINETY MINUTES from Tokyo by electric train, Nippon City is located within the sprawling Kanto Plain. Today, large portions of the Japanese population live in similar circumstances, close to modern urban centers of industry and commerce, but not a part of them. Surrounded by the irrigated paddy fields that have dominated the Japanese landscape for about two thousand years, Nippon City is a combination of traditional and modern influences, economies, and ways of life. Serviced by an efficient system of public transportation, Nippon City and other similar communities are in close contact with the modern urban social patterns of Japan's major cities. The assimilation process, however, is far from complete.

Any study of a Japanese community—from the most modern sections of Tokyo to the most backward of isolated mountain villages—must consider the combination of traditional and modern influences on people's lives and the institutional patterns of their communities. In a situation where many styles of life exist together, however, the range of possible adaptations to the modern Japanese scene are most easily seen.

The Nippon City railroad station stands near the center of the city and faces a large public square. Three bus companies use the square as a terminus for fifty-seven different routes which fan out from the urban population center to the surrounding countryside which is included within the city limits. The total population of Nippon City is 70,000, of whom 25,000 live in the central urban section. The other 45,000 people live in scattered smaller residential groupings within the city limits, separated from the central urban section and each other by farm and forest land.

A three-story branch of a major Tokyo department store dominates one side of the public square. In the Tokyo fashion there is a specialty food shop on the ground floor and a children's amusement park and observation tower on the roof. The display windows usually feature the latest in Western women's fashions.

Farther around the square, one sees various smaller establishments including two small shops that furnish bicycle and motorcycle parking services for Tokyo-bound commuters. In a city where one-tenth of the employed population finds work in the vicinity of Tokyo and about five hundred students commute regularly to school in Tokyo, such businesses are by no means marginal. Wealthier commuters and visitors are served by the taxi stands located next to the bicycle stands. Private automobiles are rare. Motorcycles are the standard form of middle class transportation.

Buses departing from the square travel along Station Avenue, a long, winding street more than a kilometer (about six tenths of a mile) in length. The commercial center of Nippon City stretches along this street which is lined on both sides with a wide variety of stalls, large and small shops, supermarkets, arcades, amusement palaces, banks, and inns. The modern white collar worker and the traditional farmer can find the merchandise or services they need somewhere along Station Avenue or its side streets.

At the far end of Station Avenue, about a kilometer from the station, are the seats of government, both ancient and modern. A two-story, dilapidated frame building houses the Nippon City Hall and Fire Department. Farther down the block is a building which houses regional representatives of the prefectural government who have responsibility for the region of which Nippon City is the center. Across the street is the site of a feudal lord's castle with moat, drum tower, and some of the gardens still extant. The center of government, up to about a hundred years ago, the castle site is now a pleasant city park with athletic fields, a small zoo, children's play area, and a newly opened swimming pool. Depending on the season, there one can see cherry blossoms surrounding the moat, an annual chrysanthemum show, or a special exhibition match of Western-style professional wrestling.

Beyond the park, a well-paved national highway runs through the city on a path parallel to the railroad tracks. It follows a historical route of the Edo Period (*ca.* 1600 to 1868) used by the feudal lords on their annual pilgrimages to Edo, now known as Tokyo. The section of the highway that once wound through the center of the city has been rerouted in recent years to run outside the old castle grounds. Straight, high-speed grades lead up to the plateaus on either side of the wide valley which Nippon City straddles.

The sides of the valley, which are raised plateaus about two and a half kilometers apart, were shorelines of a prehistoric lake that once covered the valley floor. The valley floor, outside the sharply defined nucleus of urban development, is covered with irrigated paddy fields, separated by small dikes into plots that are owned and farmed by individual households.

The farmers do not live among the field plots, but in small residential *buraku* (hamlets) of fifteen or more houses. They farm a series of small plots, usually scattered in different locations.

On top of the plateaus, upland dry fields and forested areas predominate while irrigated paddy fields have been developed along the banks of small streams or in low-lying areas.

One would gather from the description above that the word "city" does not have the same meaning as it does in the United States. In Japan, for the purposes of local government, the total area of each *ken* (prefecture) has been divided into geographic sections called *shi* (city), *machi* (town), and *mura* (village). In spite of the commonly used English translations given above, none of the terms refers to the residential units called cities, towns, and villages in America or England. In Japan, they are geographical subdivisions, so arranged that all land area of a *ken* is included in one or another of the divisions. The major difference between political units given these classifications is one of total population, though it generally holds that the cities have a larger percentage of urban population and a higher proportion of inhabitants engaged in urban occupations than towns or villages. Almost all cities, however, include a substantial segment of rural population and farmland, while towns and villages may have some urban sections.

The map of Nippon City at the front of this book shows the location of urban and rural residential areas, the main highway, the railroad, and other geographical features. Directly north of the central nucleus of urban development, and still on the valley floor, is an adjacent area of urban development backed up against the plateau. Connected to the central nucleus by a narrow link of urban development along the old route of the national highway, the urban center of Tokai Town was once a competing center of urban commercial development. From it agricultural *buraku* stretch out in each direction along the plateau.

North and west of Tokai Town, covering a large area of land, is the most sparsely populated part of the city, primarily agricultural in nature. Between Tokai Town and the city's urban center are paddy fields and the extensive site of a sewer pipe factory, the largest factory in the city. Though the north side of the city is primarily agricultural area, all parts of the city have farm population, including the outer edges of the urban center. Where urban developments have infringed on once rural hamlets, agricultural and non-agricultural families often continue to live side by side, making it difficut to clearly separate urban and rural districts. Many families are involved in both agricultural and nonagricultural work. A common pattern is seen in the husband going off to hold down a salaried job while the wife and other family members maintain the farm with the husband's help in his spare time.

Because of the tremendous population pressure that has been built up in Tokyo, recently bringing the official population figure over ten million for metropolitan Tokyo, national government planning officials have officially encouraged plans for the development of satellite cities around Tokyo which will help attract new industrial developments and other organizations. Nippon City has been so designated.

According to a recent description, the plans for Nippon City development specify a drastic increase in the percentage of the labor force employed in manufacturing and construction categories (from 14 to 40 percent) while maintaining a stable agricultural work force. Because of an anticipated population amounting to three times the present level, however, the percentage of agricultural workers will drop from 29 to 10 percent of the employed labor force.

Other aspects of the development plans go well beyond industrial development. Plans are already underway for a private university to move its campus from Tokyo to Nippon City; facilities were built for a part of the 1964 Olympic Games that were centered in Tokyo; and a large amusement park to attract tourists is in progress.

One of the first phases of the city's development plans to be realized was the beginning of construction of a major factory located on the plateau behind Tokai Town.

Nippon City is the larger environment of the local community in this study. Within the city limits, there are five middle schools serving the different sections of the city. The Nichū Middle School District, in the northwestern corner of the city, is the local community in the following discussion. Since the district is affiliated as a political and social unit with Nippon City, continuing reference to the wider community will be necessary.

THE NICHŪ MIDDLE SCHOOL DISTRICT

The Nichū School District is composed of two local communities: largely urban Tokai Town and rural Uena Region. These formerly independent political units were amalgamated with Nippon City in 1940 and 1947 respectively. In April, 1949, they were connected for the purpose of forming a middle school district. The Nichū Middle School is the major formal organization that presently unites Tokai Town with Uena Region, outside their common affiliation with Nippon City. In keeping with their identity as separate sections of the city, separate post offices, agricultural cooperatives, and elementary schools are maintained.

There is a greater sense of solidarity among the residents of Tokai Town, particularly those who live in the urban center, than among the residents of Uena Region. The Tokai people live in closer proximity to each other and have a longer history of joint action as a political and social unit.

Symbolic of Tokai Town unity is the central Shinto shrine which is considered to serve the area within the former town limits. Representatives from each section of the town who are responsible for financing and management of the shrine form a shrine wardens organization (*cf.* Dore 1958: 296–97). In 1962, an elaborate stone memorial to the town's men killed in World War II was erected. Included in the names inscribed on the back were men from Tokai Town, but none from Uena Region.

There is no central Shinto shrine for the Uena Region. Instead, there are several local shrines. Indeed, throughout both Tokai Town and Uena Region there are many smaller Shinto shrines, some identified with a specific area and others which are not.

The major difference between Tokai Town and Uena Region is the different proportion of people engaged in agriculture. Uena Region is mainly a rural agricultural area, while Tokai Town is much more of an urban settlement with its residents engaged in a variety of occupations. The number of people employed in manufacturing in Tokai Town is significantly higher than the overall Nippon City average and is attributable to the presence of a sewer pipe factory within Tokai Town which is owned by a local business man, very conscious of his social ties to Tokai Town.

Outside of the Station Avenue shopping district, neighborhood shops are located in the front rooms of the owners' houses and are one-family operations. Even the larger shops in Tokai Town are extensions of the owners' living quarters. Small manufacturing plants are conducted on the same basis, including a large Tokai Town metal-working machine shop that is located directly next to the owner-operator's house with the owner and his eldest son performing most of the work.

The people of Uena Region live in widely scattered *buraku* groups and tend to identify themselves with their *buraku*. This is also true of the Tokai Town residents who live in the two agricultural *buraku* that were included under the *machi* government before amalgamation with Nippon City.

The *buraku* are recognized by the city government for census purposes. Nichū District *buraku* sections include from 25 to 400 households each. While *buraku* are commonly contiguous settlements of rural households, usually engaged in agriculture, the census-defined *buraku* often consist of several smaller non-contiguous settlements joined for convenience into a larger unit. The smaller settlements are also called *buraku* by the people involved. Such a *buraku* is a "clearly defined social community . . . [whose] inhabitants have a strong sense of group identity" (Beardsley, Hall, and Ward 1959:4).

In the urban section of Tokai Town, ambiguously referred to as Tokai, there are eight census-defined *ku* (ward) districts, that function in similar ways to the rural *buraku*. Two of these *ku* are partly agricultural as well as urban.

The *ku* districts are numbered and are not usually referred to by name. They are known as the first *ku* of Tokai Machi, etc.

The Uena Region, like other Japanese rural areas, has many urban features. The Japanese farm family lives close to its neighbors in a compact neighborhood. The density of rural population means that many of the amenities of urban life are easily extended to rural areas. For instance, the Uena homes have all been electrified for a long time. City style bus service reaches all *buraku*. The media of mass communication reaches all homes. Almost everyone has access to a TV set, as well as a radio, in his own house or in that of a neighbor. Twice daily, deliveries of national newspapers reach all homes whose families have the small price of a subscription. The influence of urban patterns and values is evident everywhere.

The authors of *Village Japan* noticed "a trend toward identification with modern, urban ways" (Beardsley, Hall, and Ward 1959:95) in the rural area which they studied. They also point to some of the underlying elements that link the urban city dweller's way of life to that of the rural areas. The intensive agricultural practices of Japanese farmers make for a "compression of population" that is reflected in both rural and urban patterns of living. Likewise, "the low value set on human time" can be seen in the very low price of an urban haircut or the long hours of intensive hard labor that go into rural rice production. Perhaps "what exists as a whole way of life in the rural community is only one layer of city life," as the *Village Japan* authors suggested (1959:2–3). However, in reverse fashion, the urban way of life is infringing on rural patterns.

SOME ASPECTS OF SOCIAL STRUCTURE

At the level of a local community in Japan, it is still true that the basic unit of society perceived by the people is the household, not the individual. A resident will describe the size of his *buraku* by the number of households. In the eyes of his neighbors, a person is viewed more as a member of a particular household than as a particular individual.

The household, called *ie* in Japanese, is a socially defined unit, fixed by long tradition. The word *ie* also refers to a stem family. In Nichū District, as in most parts of Japan, it usually consists of a patrilineal, patrilocal family line. The predecessors in the family line, whether living or dead, are very much a part of the *ie* which continues through time . . . with changing personnel but an unchanging "identity" (Dore 1958:99). While households generally include the living members of a single stem family, some members may reside elsewhere.

In ideal form within an agricultural setting, the *ie* and its property, including farmland and house, are operated as a single social and economic unit with the co-operative labor of adult family members. The ancestors' presence is represented by tablets bearing the death name of each deceased *ie* ancestor, which are displayed in the household's cupboard-like Buddhist altar. The eldest son, as the inheritor of the family line, begins to work with his father in the fields when he is through with his formal education. His wife and children will be regular family members, with the wife making a formal transfer from the *ie* of her birth to the *ie* of her husband at the time of marriage. Thus, a wife marries *into* a family rather than merely establishing a special relationship with her husband.

When the older generation grandfather and grandmother decide to turn over the heavy work and the headship of the *ie* to their eldest son or successor they may retire and move into a retirement house or wing in close proximity to their successors. The family kitchen and bath will probably still accommodate them. For long periods of time, however, two adult generations of the family will be living and working together in all family affairs.

Unmarried children of both adult couples may continue to be an integral part of the *ie* and its life. Mature daughters will, if possible, be married off and enter the families of their husbands. Second sons, including all sons except the eldest, have several possibilities. They may marry into an *ie* which does not have a son to continue the family line. In that case, they will be adopted husbands and will take the names of their wives, becoming in many respects, the eldest sons of their new households. Alternatively, the *ie* may decide that it is wealthy enough to establish a second son and his wife as a new branch household (*bunke*) with a share of the family farmland and a new house. In so doing, a new *ie* is born, though it carries a direct relation to the main house (*honke*) from which it originated. A *bunke* also can be established for a daughter and her husband, in which case the husband is adopted into the family and takes the family name, but does not become the inheritor of the family line (*ie*). A third possibility for non-inheriting second sons, and the most common practice in Nichū District, is to establish them in a new urban occupation. Generally, formal education at a higher level is viewed as a desirable path for establishing such sons in a new occupation, but even those who do not go beyond their compulsory education can easily find jobs in the city. The demand for middle school graduates by various employers was 2.7 times the number of children available in 1962 (*Japan Times,* Sept. 17, 1962). If they do not continue their education after middle school graduation, both girls and boys will look for work in Nippon City, Tokyo, or elsewhere.

Second sons will, as a rule, leave their natal home for the industry and commerce of Tokyo which has continued to absorb, during the century of modern development, the surplus rural population of the Kanto Plain. Thus they establish a new household. In Nippon City, convenient to Tokyo, such sons can be given a house in the community to establish a *bunke* without farmland. Girls who go to work will return to their homes after a few years to prepare for marriage.

A common concern of the Japanese farm family has been the orderly continuation of the *ie*. For prosperous farm families, this has not been difficult, because even childless couples could adopt children as their *atotsugi* (one who succeeds to the family line.) For poorer families, whose resources might be overtaxed in supporting two adult couples and the various unmarried children involved, the problem of family continuation has often been desperate and insoluble. In many cases the answer is to send the *atotsugi* eldest son to work in the city with the understanding that he will return to the farm when his parents are ready to retire or to establish the "weekend and womenfolk" (Dore 1959:276) farming pattern. In the latter case, the head of the household has a salaried job and leaves the management of the farm to his wife although he helps with the heavy work on weekends.

Because the *ie* is also a system of social security for the elderly family members, *ie*-continuation is a vital concern of the parental and grandparental generations. Such concern is reflected in the patterns of childrearing. Foreign observers, at least those who have had a chance for extended first-hand observation, inevitably comment on the permissiveness of the family toward its children. Physical punishment of any kind is extremely rare. The whole family strives to communicate affection for the child. Patience and forebearance are notable qualities of the average Japanese mother. Throughout the many social activities of the household, as in the social activities of the society at large, there is a constant concern for the individual's feelings. A mother or grandmother attempting to persuade a small boy from some destructive or dangerous action will inevitably say, "You're a good boy (*oriko*)." One never hears, "You're a bad boy," or "Bad boys do that, but good boys don't."

While toilet training begins early, it is not severe and consists of holding a baby out over the side of the porch when the mother expects him to perform. The author's wife was shocked to see her six-month-old son being held in such a way over the porch edge by the elderly lady who helped care for the baby. The important point is that there was no severity.

The concern for a person's feelings (*kimochi*) carries over to an adult level. The first topic of conversation at most drinking parties attended by the author was "How are your feelings?" That question immediately followed the first two thimblefulls of *sake*. The explanation of the question was that the purpose of such parties is to develop good feelings among the participants. Indeed, it was a most effective device for this purpose since social patterns of drunkenness, brought on by very little actual consumption of alcohol, involved conviviality without aggression or friction.

Through a variety of practices, the Japanese family has managed to reduce intergenerational friction to a tolerable level and has inculcated *ie* loyalty so that many households exist as truly cooperative social units with three or even four generations included in their composition.

The above description of the household has concentrated on the ideal pattern of the household in a rural setting. However, rural values have carried over to urban society. Eldest sons enter into and carry on their father's business or trade, in the same way that rural youth enter agriculture. Even the modern son of a salaried company employee may continue living at home though usually working for a separate company.

Postwar innovations have affected the workings of the family system, which is still, however, held as an ideal, particularly in rural areas. Land reform programs of the American Occupation decreed that no one could own more land than he was farming with his household. This reduced all landlords to the economic status of working farmers. Innovations in farming techniques, particularly the introduction of weed-killing chemicals, extensive use of chemical fertilizers, and the introduction of machinery useful in the small-scale farming pattern of Japan, have drastically reduced the hours of labor needed to maintain a family farm. From this later development has arisen the possibility of "weekend and womenfolk" farming.

Adult family members, usually the younger men who have acquired more education than their fathers, can hold a full-time job in Tokyo or elsewhere, and still keep the family farm going. First sons no longer have to consider farming as their life occupation. It is a common observation of middle school officials in the whole Kanto Plain area that first sons are no longer separable from second sons in their desire to continue their education beyond the compulsory level to a high school education. Higher education is desired by all as a path to economically better jobs regardless of one's *atotsugi* responsibilities. A better life can be gained, while fulfilling one's responsibilties for *ie* continuation.

Postwar changes in the legal system have taken away the legal props of the traditional family system, particulary in a requirement that family property inheritance be split among all children. Though the law does not require that farm landholdings be split up, there is growing concern for the rights of non-inheriting sons. In practice, it is impossible to split farm landholdings and a house that are barely sufficient to maintain the first son's family. Financing of higher education for second sons is perceived as an alternate form of inheritance that gives such sons the ability to establish themselves in a new occupation in much the same manner that the eldest son is established in agriculture. It is also a common occurrence for a second son to inherit the family farm through disinclination on the part of the first son to carry on the family line and occupation.

The lowest level of official political organization in which people vote for representatives and an administrative officer is the *shi* (city), *machi* (town), or *mura* (village). There are no election districts within such a unit, so that city, town, or village assembly members are elected at large. In practice, in a place like Nippon City, there is a good deal of informal preliminary political arranging in which the formerly independent *machi* and *mura* areas agree on a candidate or candidates whom they will support and have enough votes to elect.

In spite of the formal, official dominance of the city government, there is a well-organized system of informal *buraku-ku* government. Such units are dealt with by the city government. The locally-selected section chief (*kuchō*) and council help to mediate between the local residents and the city government. It is in the selection of such local officers that informal tradition plays a more important part than the officially-proclaimed postwar political structure.

Local men of influence (*yūryokusha*) form the local councils or arrange for the selection of men who will look after the interests of the community (Ike 1957:75). These are the same people who will be involved with the selection of district candidates for the city assembly. In the Nichū District, many of the *yūryokusha* have prewar landlord connections. Connections with a prominent family of long-standing in the district or nearby areas would seem essential to achievement of such status. One "young" man of forty-two from one of the most remote farm villages was a *yūryokusha* of the Uena Region because he was the family head of the *ie* which had been the largest landholder of the area before the American Occupation instituted land reform. Graduate of a prewar merchant marine training school, he had been called back to the village after the war to take over the headship of a related family with no children. Modern in education and orientation, it was his family status that placed him in a position of authority, though his family fortunes had declined greatly due to the land reform program. He and his wife were now full-time farmers.

Another *yūryokusha* given a prominent place at local functions of the Nichū District was the direct descendant of the family which had furnished the principle retainer for the Nippon City castle's lord in pre-modern times.

A leading *yūryokusha* of the Nichū District was a second son of a prewar landlord family who had not succeeded formally to being head of that family and had not received more than a low-prestige, private, prewar middle school education. Locally reputed to be one of those who financed the mayor's election campaigns, he was a businessman who had started and developed his own business, the Nippon City sewer pipe factory. He presently owns several factories in different parts of Japan. Described by a long time local teacher as a man "who did not like politics," he has not run for or held elective political office. But he was president of the Nippon City Chamber of Commerce and Industry, vice president of the prefectural organization of the same name, chairman of the shrine wardens organization for the Tokai Town shirine, chairman of the Nichū Middle School PTA for thirteen years, chairman of the most prestigious Ichikō High School's PTA, and the man most likely to be named as the chairman of any new organization formed in the Nichū District. The two new organizations formed in 1962 each elected him as chairman. One was a fan-club group formed to support a local Uena Region boy who made good as a professional baseball player on a prominent national team. The other organization was set up to discuss and promote local solutions for problems dealing with juvenile delinquency.

While probably chairman in name only of some of his organizations, he appeared on ceremonial or public occasions involving the organizations and visibly enjoyed the signs of status to which his various positions entitled him. Not an example of traditional leadership, in an area where leadership is usually much more discreet and self-effacing, he was a home-town boy who had good family connections and had made his way in the business world. Though his business extended over large parts of the nation, it was in the local leadership of local organizations that he validated his accomplishments and derived his pleasures. The obvious possessor of a good deal of wealth, he used it for conspicuous local contribution rather than personal conspicuous consumption. Puritanical in his emphasis upon family simplicity, he did not provide a maid for his wife to help with the housework in their simple home. Conspicuous contributions included five million yen ($14,000) for a new middle school gymnasium, which his company contracted with the city to build; the same amount for restoration of the Tokai elementary school; a smaller amount for the construction of a new industrial high school in the Nichū District; and a larger amount for scholarship funds to be used for encouragement of industrial high school students in all of the areas where his factories were located.

The general attributes of *yūryokusha* (man of influence) status seemed to be (1) good local family connections, (2) connection with prewar landlord status in rural areas, (3) commercial success and connections, (4) age, and (5) ability. Not all of these qualifications had to be met, but the more the better for giving local prestige and status.

A more modern form of local leadership and access to *yūryokusha* status, through education and professional standing, is exemplified by the doctor who lives and practices medicine in East Nami *buraku* (Uena). In spite of the harried life of a general practitioner with patients coming to him at all hours, he manges to find time to be active in many positions of local influence. Chairman of the elementary school PTA, one of the organizers of the new association to support the local baseball champion, and vice-chairman of the Nichū PTA are a few of the posts he holds.

Beside those *yūryokusha* who hold the publicly prestigious formal positions, there are others who make their influence felt behind the scenes. The same requirements for *yūryokusha* status stated above hold for these men, but they are more difficult for a foreign investigator connected with the middle school to get to know. It is not valid, however, to dismiss those who take the public honors of *yūryokusha* status as mere "front men." Both types of leaders obviously wield local political and social power.

For purposes of comparison, it is significant that Japanese investigators in southern Japan, concerned with the relationship of the local political power structure to educational organizations in a rural area, found that the positions of leadership in local community organizations were considered to be, and were, in fact, stepping stones to formal political office as elective assembly members or appointive members of the board of education (Yano 1961).

The Nichū Middle School, however, is not only an institution of the local community; it is also one segment of a formal school system that links together with other schools in a number of significant ways. In the next chapter we explore these linkages in the school system with an emphasis on historical development and the ways in which Nippon City children are channeled through the system.

2 / The local school system

NICHŪ DISTRICT SCHOOLS

SEPARATE ELEMENTARY SCHOOLS (*shōgakkō*) serve Tokai Town and Uena Region. The Tokai Elementary School was established around 1879, but the present buildings and site date back sixty years. This has been long enough for the ornamental cherry trees that were planted in the school's playground to have fully matured. With the special care that these trees have received, they have grown magnificently and have been designated for protection by the prefectural government. The care of the trees is symbolic of the community's long concern for the school.

The school is located on the edge of the plateau, overlooking the city, and is immedately adjacent to the Tokai Town Shrine. Though recently renovated, the old frame buildings are in need of paint. Until the end of the war, most community residents did not continue their education beyond this elementary school. Thus the school is still important as the highest school attended by a large number of community residents and leaders. An active alumni organization includes graduates who have moved away from Nippon City to other parts of Japan. Along with the PTA, it helps in raising substantial funds needed to supplement the regular school budget and to provide new facilities for the pupils.

The Uena Elementary School is a country school. Located in the midst of farm fields, it began forty-five years ago as a consolidated elementary school, replacing four previous schools which had served the decentralized rural *buraku*. There is no active alumni organization in this school. Even though there is a large semi-urban *buraku* in its district, the school is classed by many people as inferior to the urban school in Tokai Town. The principal says that his children are not able to express themselves as well as the town children, and the farm families do not exert pressure for their children to study in the way that the town parents do. Some ambitious Uena Region parents try to find ways to get their children into the Tokai School, rather than the Uena School.

Though even young children come a long distance to attend the Uena School, there is a school rule that they must walk. Auto and truck traffic on the country roads makes bicycle riding dangerous, and the rural bus schedules do not conform with the school schedule. For some children, it is a one-hour walk between school and home.

Both elementary schools enroll children in the first grade if they are already six years old by the opening of the school year at the beginning of April. There are no public *yōchien* (kindergartens) in the Nichū District, but there is a private *hoikuen* (nursery school) in Tokai Town that many children attend for one to three years before going to elementary school. Only a few children from Uena Region attend the nursery school, though many Tokai Town urban children attend. A few children ride the bus to town every day and attend public or private *yōchien* in other parts of Nippon City. While a large number of Tokai Elementary School children have had kindergarten or nursery school experience, the Uena School children generally have not. Kindergartens in Nippon City do not generally include an introduction to academic work, though they do provide an introduction to group activity in a classroom situation.

Children are grouped in heterogeneous classes in both elementary schools, except that the Tokai School does have a special classroom for very retarded children where they are given six years of specialized schooling. The elementary school teachers point out that it is somewhat ironic for the very formal room, once reserved for the Emperor's portrait and the school's official copy of the Imperial Rescript on Education, to be converted now into a classroom for about sixteen retarded children. The Uena School does not have such a class and any retarded students are merely distributed among the regular class groups. They are not allowed to attend the special class in the Tokai School.

Both schools are large enough to have two or more class sections at each grade level. All children, regardless of achievement, retardation, or even school attendance, are promoted each year with their age-mates to the next grade. After six years of elementary schooling, *all* children, including those in the Tokai School's special class, are graduated and passed on to Nichū Middle School (*chūgakkō*).

Once they enter Nichū, children will continue to participate in groups based on residence for certain school-related recreational activities. Their class assignments will be strictly random, both by residence and ability. There is no special class at Nichū for the retarded children.

Nichū provides three final years of compulsory education to all graduates of the two elementary schools and the few newcomers to the Nichū District who are the proper age. Upon graduation from the middle school, children are free to apply for entrance to high schools, (*kōtō gakkō*), look for jobs, or stay home. All children of the appropriate age-range in the district are enrolled at Nichū. Graduation diplomas are refused only to those few who have failed to meet the attendance requirements. Any student who attends school faithfully, regardless of comprehension or achievement, will receive a diploma.

The importance of school attendance for evaluating a child's accomplishments was commented on by a writer in premodern times. "A student who attends regularly is rewarded even if he is of only average ability, whereas even an outstandingly good pupil, if he does not attend regularly, be he never so admirably behaved and accomplished, will never be given a prize" (Quoted in Dore 1965:181).

Of 275 pupils who completed their compulsory education requirements in April, 1962, at Nichū, seven did not receive diplomas. Two of these had never attended junior high school, one because she was chronically ill and one because she had to help at home. One boy attended the opening ceremony on the first day of school, but never came again. "He couldn't find his way home by himself," said a teacher describing the boy's retardation. Two attended some time, but did not come at all during their third year (ninth grade). The other two managed to come to school less than half the time throughout their school career, though they did show up for at least a part of their third-year's work. Pupils with a complete record of failure in their academic work were given diplomas if they did not have an abnormal rate of absence. No one was enrolled for more than three years.

Studies conducted in other communities have consistently noted this same feature of Japanese schools, in that all pupils are promoted and graduated automatically, from any school to which they are admitted.

> Though the children undergo periodic tests, they almost invariably are promoted each year and so stay with the same group of schoolmates, with whom they form friendships that endure through life. Teachers in lower (elementary) and middle school almost never inflict on a child the shame of failure, which would be reflected on the child's family and buraku, so the slow children pass through school at the same rate as the bright ones (Beardsley, Hall, and Ward 1959:302).

> Teachers feel that, if they left some child behind his class, he would feel very badly about it and that the resulting psychological effect and family chagrin would not be compensated for by any good the child might receive mentally by repeating a school grade (Embree 1939:188).

The same reasons are given by Nichū District teachers for their promotion policy. It is important to note the second quotation above comes from Embree's prewar Japanese community study indicating that the practice of automatic promotion is not a recent introduction. In fact, Dore feels that automatic promotion and age-grading was the device used by pre-Meiji schools for *samurai* to escape ordering of pupils by their hereditary rank (1965:180–86).

The Nichū Middle School is housed in rambling frame buildings, the first of which were erected soon after the end of World War II. Small flowering cherry trees planted along the edge of the school yard show, by comparison with the Tokai Elementary School, the relative newness of the school. It is pleasantly located on the edge of the plateau overlooking Tokai Town and the urban nucleus of Nippon City on the valley floor below. Only a short distance from the Tokai Elementary School, the Nichū-Middle School is easily reached by the children who live in Tokai Town. However, the Uena Region children find it difficult to get to school. Long, covered bicycle racks between the two rows of classrooms give ample evidence of the most common method of getting to school. Some children come from Uena Region by regular city bus. Those children living in the farthest hamlets of Uena Region need about forty minutes to bicycle to school in good weather.

Ichikō High School, Kōkō Industrial High School, and the Industrial Training Center are also located geographically within the Nichū District, but are by no means limited to Nichū District students. The high schools are administered directly by the Prefectural Board of Education and furnish three years of secondary education to students from a large part of the prefecture who are able to pass the difficult entrance examination requirements.

The Industrial Training Center is administered by the Ministry of Labor, through a prefectural office. It offers a one-year, non-academic training program which leads to qualification for a variety of industrial occupations, depending on the particular courses taken. Both boys and girls are enrolled in the program. Though the buildings are immediately adjacent to the Kōkō Industrial High School, the two schools have no official connection nor do they share facilities. About 90 percent of the Center's students are junior high school graduates. The rest are high school graduates or older workers being retrained for new jobs.

In March 1962, 275 pupils finished their compulsory education at Nichū Middle School. Of these, 173 pupils or about 63 percent went on to high school. Only 41 pupils were able to enter high schools in Nichū District; about one-fourth of those going on to high school. Among these, 18 boys and 2 girls were admitted to Ichikō High School, and 7 boys went on to Kōkō Industrial High School. Nine boys and five girls were admitted to the night school section of Ichikō High School, a four-year academic program for students employed during the day. In addition, ten boys and five girls were admitted to the Industrial Training Center. Thus, while these schools are physically located in the Nichū District, they have only a few students from the district and little direct connection with the local community, except as one segment of the large area from which they draw their students.

BEFORE AND AFTER THE WAR

The school system, as described above, developed after the war. It has been in operation for less than twenty years. Parents of middle school students and community leaders are, therefore, products of the prewar educational system. In order to understand their attitudes about education and the schools today, it is necessary to know something about the prewar schools.

Before 1941, the period of compulsory education was six years of elementary schooling. Because this has been so since 1908 (Anderson 1959:34), only the oldest residents of Nichū District have less than a six-year elementary school education. In fact, the largest number of residents participated in a voluntary extension of the elementary school program called *kōtō shōgakkō* (higher elementary school). This was a two-year, full-time program conducted at the elementary school for all who desired to participate. In the nation as a whole, 67 percent of the children went on to *kōtō shōgakkō*, (Anderson 1959:34) and Nichū District was not exceptional in this pattern. Beyond the *kōtō shōgakkō*, there were youth schools or classes (*seinen gakkō*) that were carried out on a part-time or full-time basis at the elementary schools. These schools, controlled closely by the National Ministry of Education as were all schools at that time, were located in the local communities and were designed, in fact, to train children for life in their home community. Specially trained teachers gave both a vocational and a moral-civics emphasis to these courses, with agriculture being stressed in rural communities. In 1931, attendance at the youth classes was made compulsory for children under nineteen years of age who had not entered the academic tracks of secondary education (Anderson 1959:40–41).

Prewar Nichū District residents had several paths of secondary education open to them. Though the majority went on in the *kōtō shōgakkō-seinen gakkō* track described above, a few went on into academic or vocational secondary education tracks. Regardless of vocational or academic emphasis, the secondary schools for boys were referred to in Nichū District as *chūgakkō* (middle school), the same word used for the postwar middle school based on the American junior high school pattern. Secondary schools for girls were the *kōtō jogakkō* (higher girls' school). These schools were the prestigious channels of education and led to higher status, depending on both the type of education and the higher education channels to which they might lead.

For Nichū District, the academic *chūgakkō,* available to boys, was the school that is now Ichikō High School. It was then, and still is, a strictly academic school, often leading to higher educational channels. After six or more years of elementary school, children could take the entrance examinations for the *chūgakkō.* The *chūgakkō* provided five more years of education and led to higher academic or technical education.

Those desiring more intensive education in agriculture than that afforded by the *seinen gakkō* would apply to an agricultural *chūgakkō* located about ten miles from Nippon City. It had a three-year, full-time academic-vocational program.

The girls who wanted more academic instruction would take the examinations for the Nippon City Kōtō Jogakkō, which is now the girl's Nikō High School in the center of Nippon City. It provided three years of academic and home economics education.

A further possibility for both boys and girls was the teacher training school in the prefectural capital, which would accept graduates of *chūgakkō* or *kōtō jogakkō.*

There were rigorous entrance examinations for academic secondary education, as there are now for high school entrance. Only the best students could hope to gain entrance.

At graduation from elementary school, children were channeled into an educational track that would determine their future role at the same time that the schools were preparing them for that role. Elementary school graduation was a time for commitment and decision. One factor that helped to make secondary academic education more available to those who desired it, and had the economic resources to continue in school, was that there were few applicants for the *chūgakkō* and *kōtō jogakkō.*

THE MIDDLE SCHOOL

Now, after World War II, the school system has changed. The prewar schools continue to function alongside new ones that have been designed to fill out the needs of the new system as well as a growing school-age population. The most radical organizational change from the former system of compulsory education is the addition of the new middle school as a separate institution. Using the name *chūgakkō* in Japanese, it is housed in a new building in a new location. Educationally, it fulfills the former role of the *kōtō shōgakkō,* as well as the prewar *chūgakkō,* in that it enrolls all children for three years of compulsory education. At the same time, it is expected to be a part of the system of secondary education, unlike the *kōtō shōgakkō* of prewar times. While some residents are honored that their children are now able to go on to the *chūgakkō,* a name that carries prestigious connotations, others are disappointed that the rigorous academic education of the former *chūgakkō,* designed for an elite student body, seems to be diluted in the postwar compulsory education version of the *chūgakkō.*

THE HIGH SCHOOLS

Postwar high schools are often housed in and are the continuation of the prewar *chūgakkō.* To a large extent, they perform the same community function that they did under the prewar system. Ichikō High School, formerly the Nippon City Chūgakkō, continues as a highly selective, elite channel to social advancement through an exclusive, academically oriented educational program that opens the doors to even more elite higher educational channels. With more than half of its graduates going on to college or a university, Ichikō has the reputation of being one of the better academic high schools in the prefecture. It is located on the national highway very close to the Tokai Elementary School and Nichū. The buildings were erected in 1905, though the school had been started earlier in a different location. The original buildings show the influence of New England school architecture on Japanese school construction of that period. In sharp contrast to the decrepit frame buildings that are still used today, a modern reinforced concrete library building was built for the school three years ago.

The children who are able to enter Ichikō get three years of rigorous academic instruction, most of it aimed at preparing them for the difficult entrance examinations of Japan's best colleges and universities. According to the results of the high school entrance examinations, the top fifty Ichikō students, and the second fifty, are separated into special homogenous class groups for more concentrated academic effort while the rest of the students are mixed together without further ability separation for their class groups. In their third year, students unable economically to consider applying for higher education are put into a separate vocational class group and given some special instruction and guidance for finding jobs.

Though Ichikō High School admitted no girls to this channel of social mobility before the war, postwar compliance with the principle of coeducation has meant a token admission of girls to the program. In 1962–1963, there were 72 girls among 1,123 students.

Entrance to Ichikō High School, as the path to prestigious higher education, is the goal of many ambitious Nichū District parents for their sons. Only rarely is it considered appropriate for girls, unless they aspire to enter first-class higher education in channels that are still considered distinctly unfeminine. Most girls, regardless of academic excellence, are interested in the Nikō High School, a school reserved exclusively for girls.

Because Ichikō now gives three, rather than five years of secondary education, more students can be accommodated in the prewar *chūgakkō* facilities. The only new construction since the war has been the school library and assembly hall, so there has been no further attempt to widen this channel of social mobility.

A postwar night school provides additional secondary educational opportunity, but performs a very different social role than the daytime program. The night school opens few doors to higher education; it is attended largely by very low-level students who have been unable to gain admission elsewhere; and it tends to be terminal education. It gives a secondary academic education to children who would have been enrolled in prewar *seinen gakkō*. Although the prefectural high school entrance examination is required of applicants, no one is refused entrance to the night school course. Boys and girls attend in approximately equal numbers.

The Nikō High School is located on the edge of the urban nucleus of Nippon City. Formerly the Nippon City Kōtō Jogakkō (higher girls' school), it continues as a completely feminine institution with no male enrollment. As before the war, it gives education for girls that is considered desirable when one begins to search for a bride. Since brides are sought more often by parents of the intended groom, than the groom himself, the Nikō education carries much the same kind of prestige that it did before the war. "The school is a signboard," said the rural parents of a girl applying for admission to Nikō. "She will be able to make a much better marriage if she has been able to get a Nikō education."

While anyone may take the prefectural high school entrance examination and apply to the high school of his choice, community feelings, self-restraint, and the entrance examinations are the major forces that keep Ichikō and Nikō in their prewar roles. While academically talented girls would always be accepted at Ichikō, they would normally choose to avoid the unfeminine education offered there unless they planned to qualify for entrance to a top university. Similarly, no boy would ever think of applying for the feminine secondary education that Nikō offers, though its official academic curriculum follows the same guidelines as other public high schools.

In recent times, the trend has been for girls to either find jobs after completing their high school education, or to enter a regular or two-year college. Nikō is considered good preparation for career girls and junior college students as well as the brides-to-be. Most girls with outstanding academic records in their middle school work deliberately choose Nikō over Ichikō because they are not planning to try for admission to the top-ranking national universities. Depending on the results of entrance examinations, Nikō students pursue either a regular academic or home economics curriculum. The latter takes in all girls at the lower end of the test score scale and effectively separates the girls into two levels of academic ability groupings for all of their school work.

The other high school in the Nichū District, the Kōkō High School, is a specialized industrial high school for boys. Located near Ichikō on the boundary between Tokai Town and Uena Region, it was built in 1959 with a brand new campus. It is a modern structure of reinforced concrete with bright, airy classrooms and workshops. Combining vocational and academic training, Kōkō prepares students for direct entrance to skilled industrial work.

With the present Nippon City emphasis on industrial development, the students can expect to find there opportunities for employment as well as jobs in Tokyo or elsewhere. In rural families even eldest sons, who are expected to continue their family line (*ie*), see the possibility of carrying out their traditional family responsibilities while attaining a higher standard of living as industrial workers and weekend farmers. Many other boys who are anxious to qualify for good industrial jobs, but are unable economically to plan for college or university education, are attracted to the Kōkō School. There is no chance for a higher education after graduation from Kōkō, but good jobs are available. Competition for entrance is such that applicants must score almost as high on the prefectural high school entrance examination for entrance to the Kōkō School as they would for entrance to Ichikō.

Other postwar high schools without prewar *chūgakkō* connections have rarely been able to establish such a level of prestige. An example of a less-prestigious postwar high school is the Nippon City Sankō High School located on the other side of the city from Nichū. The school has both an academic as well as a commercial curriculum. Students apply for entrance to one or the other. Boys who cannot qualify for Ichikō, and girls who cannot get into Nikō, apply for entrance to the academic curriculum, along with a few students who choose the commercial curriculum. Because Sankō is more conveniently located than a number of other low-prestige high schools outside the city limits, it is the usual second choice of Nichū graduates who have to give up aspirations for Ichikō or Nikō. Unlike the Nikō separation of students by ability for the different curricula offered, Sankō allows its students, within the limitations imposed by class quotas, to select either the academic or commercial curriculum. A few students elect the commercial curriculum as a second choice when unable to qualify for the more popular academic curriculum.

Even lower on the totem pole of prestige is the Yonkō High School, about twenty miles outside Nippon City. Nichū boys and girls who cannot hope to qualify for Sankō apply at Yonkō as a last chance. The large number of applicants who *fail* the examination for entrance to Yonkō is evidence of its "last chance" status. There are three other schools of even lower rank, Rokkō, Nanakō, and Hakkō, but they are so far away that daily transportation to these schools is an almost insurmountable problem for Nichū District residents. Many Nichū graduates take the Yonkō entrance examinations as a last chance and then apply to the Ichikō night school course or to the private high schools in Nippon City and elsewhere if they fail to make the grade for Yonkō.

Since high school education is beyond the compulsory education period, Nichū graduates may choose whether they will apply for further education, look for a job, or stay at home to work with their family. Table 1 shows the number of graduates who went on to each high school, to jobs in the Tokyo area, to local jobs, or who stayed home after graduation from Nichū in March 1962. It can be seen that 73 percent of the class of 1962 went on to further education of some sort, but only 51 percent were able to enter public high schools. Of the thirty-two graduates entering private high schools, twenty-seven failed entrance examinations to one of the public schools. One boy passed the entrance examination to Rokkō High School with such a high score that he chose to attend a good private high

TABLE 1

POSTGRADUATION EDUCATION AND EMPLOYMENT
NICHŪ CLASS OF 1962

	No. of Children	Percent
Further Education		
Prestige High Schools		
Ichikō (Boyce Academic)	20	
Nikō (Girls)	40	
Kōkō (Industrial	7	
Total	67	24
Low Prestige Public Public High Schools		
Sankō (Academic and Commercial)	24	
Yonkō (Academic)	17	
Gokō (Girls)	8	
Rokkō (Agriculture)	4	
Nanakō (Academic and Agriculture)	4	
Hakkō (Agriculture)	2	
Ichikō Night School	14	
Other Night Schools	1	
Total	74	27
Private High Schools		
Nippon City Girls High School	19	
Nippon City Boys High School	3	
Out-of-town Private High Schools	10	
Total	32	12
Other Education		
Vocational Training Center	15	
Factory High Schools (*Ginōsha Yōseijo*)	6	
Barbers School	2	
Cram School (*Yobikō*)	2	
Other	3	
Total	28	10
Employment (Incl. employed night school students)		
Nippon City	26	
Within the Prefecture	3	
Tokyo	36	
Elsewhere	2	
Total	67	24

TABLE 1 (*continued*)

	No. of Children	Percent
Stay-at-home		
Farm Homes	8	
Non-farm Homes	4	
Total	12	4
Unknown	2	1
Total Graduates	268*	
Total Nongraduates (No diploma)	7	

* Because seven Ichikō Night School students are employed, they are counted twice in the table and the sub-totals add up to seven more than the 275 members of the class of 1962.

school in the prefectural capital, a long distance from his home. The other four graduates who entered private high schools did so poorly in their middle school work that they were advised by their Nichū teachers to not even try the entrance examinations of one of the public high schools.

During the postwar period there has been a noticeable decline of interest in the agricultural high school curriculum. Rokkō High School—successor of the prewar agricultural *chūgakkō* that many Nichū District residents attended—attracts very few students now. Also, very few rural children are living at home on the farms. Only eight Nichū graduates remained at home in 1962, as shown in Table 1. This does not indicate that rural children are leaving home permanently, but rather that they are (1) obtaining as much education as their qualifications permit and (2) seeking nonfarm jobs and skills away from home for a few years, returning at a later date.

For those children planning to continue their education after Nichū, admission to a public high school is in no way assured. There are insufficient facilities to accommodate all who apply. A difficult examination is designed by the Prefectural Education Office to decide who will be admitted. An important aspect of this system is the risk involved for many of the students.

Before the prefectural high school entrance examination is administered, all middle school third-year pupils (ninth graders) who wish to attend a public high school must file an application with the school of their choice. Only one application is possible because the tests are identical and administered on the same day throughout the prefecture. Before or after the examination, but not before the test results are announced, one may transfer his application to a different school. High school admissions are then announced the day *after* middle school graduation ceremonies. Those graduates who do not make the grade for the school for which they applied have three alternative routes to further education. They can (1) go to the four-year night-school course of Ichikō; (2) apply for admission to a private high school; or (3) go to a private "cram school" (*yobikō*) or to a tutor to prepare for next year's entrance examination for the school of their choice in the hope that one year's extra preparation will enable them to score satisfactorily. There is no possibility that an applicant who fails to gain admittance at Ichikō will qualify for a lower prestige, full-time public high school in the same year. For children of borderline ability, deciding on a school requires a deliberate gamble. In applying to the school of higher prestige, one risks being eliminated from entrance to *any* public high school that year. Applying to one of lower prestige means that one is sure to be admitted, but if the entrance examination results are exceptionally good, one will still have lost the chance for admission to the prestige school.

In discussing admission practices, there are some high school administrators who say that middle school records and recommendations are considered along with the test scores, but there is evidence that test scores are the major criterion of admission. Though test results and minimum passing scores for each high school are confidential, middle school teachers in Nippon City regularly compare notes and determine the lowest passing scores for Nippon City children. The high schools notify each middle school of the test results for their own pupils, so it is a relatively simple matter for the teachers to compare notes. As advisers to the children, and with a continuing responsibility for the following year's class, teachers must know the relative rankings of the high schools and the test scores required for entrance. Since all applicants are accepted by the Ichikō night course, there is no minimum score.

Justification for the system of entrance examinations is usually stated in terms of the need to minimize the effect of personal connections on high school entrance. One example of collusion on test scoring to allow a high school employee's son to enter was described to the author. However, this seems to occur very infrequently. In Japanese society, personal connections have always been considered very effective for achieving one's social or business purposes. The entrance examinations are a definite attempt to substitute an impartial, achievement-oriented system for one that would allow personal influence to be dominant.

An admissions official at one of Tokyo's major private universities described to the author his original plans to install a system for determining university entrance that was better than the similarly strict reliance on entrance examination scores. However, a fear of personal connections becoming important in an admissions policy that would depend on school records and personal recommendations, as well as on examination results, effectively kept him from adopting such a policy for the university.

Further evidence for the prestige ranking of the high schools described above is given in Table 2 which compares the postgraduation experiences of graduates of the five major high schools and the Ichikō Night School. Though Ichikō and Kōkō High Schools attract the same quality of students academically, the sharp difference in their purposes is evident in the percentage of graduates going on to higher education. The source of their prestige lies in their fulfillment of different purposes.

Of the 1962 Ichikō graduates who were going on to higher education only half were actually able to enter a university or college directly. The rest, having failed one entrance examination, would have to study for one or more years until they,

TABLE 2

POSTGRADUATION EDUCATION AND EMPLOYMENT FOR NIPPON CITY HIGH SCHOOL GRADUATES, 1962

High School	Further Education				Employed				Other		Total Graduates	Percentage of graduates to higher education[b]
	4 year college or university	2 year junior college	Other higher education	Rōnin (studying for future entrance exams)	Government	Banks and companies	Home business	Other employment	No employment or further education	Unknown		
Ichikō	158	5	2	140	10	35	8	1			359	78[b]
Nikō	63	58	40		33	238		11	16	90[a]	549	34
Sankō	29	2	16		34	110	4	62	15		272	17
Kōkō					1	150	3	1	7		162	0
Yonkō	6	3	5		3	98		16	5	30[a]	166	8
Ichikō Night School	3				5	17		15	8	15	63	5

[a] Probably includes girls who stay at home and prepare for marriage.
[b] Includes *rōnin* students.

TABLE 3

Ichikō Graduates admitted to Higher Education, 1954 to 1962

Graduating Classes	Total Graduates	Applicants to Higher Education		Year Entrance Examination Passed									Total Admitted	
		No.	Percent	1954	1955	1956	1957	1958	1959	1960	1961	1962	No.	Percent
1954	315	207	66	127	46	14	3	1	0	2			193	61
1955	333	214	64		111	66	18	6	1	1	1		204	61
1956	356	248	70			94	70	25	6	2	1		198	56
1957	350	231	66				89	67	24	6	2		188	54
1958	358	257	72					129	68	14	2		213	60
1959	350	254	73						105	81	26	8	220	63
1960	352	251	71							118	78	26	222	63
1961	360	291	81								132	73	205	57
1962	359	305	85									165	165	46

Nichū Middle School students watching activities on the school grounds.

too, could gain university admittance. Table 3 shows the length of time that some of the Ichikō graduates have had to wait for admission to higher education.

University entrance examinations are somewhat like the high school entrance examinations, but the competition is fiercer. The high number of Ichikō students who must study for a year or more beyond graduation at "cram schools" (*yobikō*) in order to pass university entrance examinations is explained by the fact that the prestige universities to which they apply have the highest numbers of applicants. Such students are called *rōnin,* a word that used to mean "masterless warrior" but now means a student waiting for entrance to a university because he has failed one or more entrance examinations.

Although high school graduate *rōnin* have been on the Japanese scene for a long time, *chūgakkō rōnin* is a pattern that is just beginning to develop. For the next few years, the pressure of students born in Japan's postwar "baby boom" on insufficient high school facilities may lead to a growing number of *chūgakkō* (middle school) graduates attending *yobikō* in order to pass their high school entrance examinations. As Professor Tokiomi Kaigo has suggested, Japan has developed a 6-3-x-3-x-4 system of education. That is, six years of elementary education, three years of junior high school education, x years of *chūgakkō rōnin* cram school, three years of high school, x years of high school *rōnin* cram school, and four years of university education (quoted in Anderson 1959:66).

Since this study is concerned primarily with the Nichū Middle School, one should note, particularly, the conflict that is inherent in the school's historical position and official *chūgakkō* title. That is, the middle school is the inheritor of two separate educational traditions. First, it is the direct replacement for the prewar *kōtō shōgakkō* (higher elementary school) which provided two years of general education, with vocational and moral, rather than academic emphasis, for a life pattern that would continue within the confines of a local community. Though no longer conducted in the elementary school building, the middle school cannot be disengaged completely from this role, since it continues to provide education for all children as an extension of their compulsory education.

Second, the middle school goes under the name *chūgakkō* in Japanese. Though it does not occupy the physical facilities of the prewar *chūgakkō,* many of which have become the prestige high schools of the postwar period, it does provide postelementary education for the children who, in prewar times, would have begun their academic secondary education separately. The middle school postpones for three more years the decision as to which educational or vocational channel one will enter, and the examinations associated with secondary school entrance.

Additionally, the postwar period of relative prosperity has led to a tremendous increase in the demand for high school admission. More than half of the post-war generation are now completing twelve years of education, and more than two thirds of the children, at a school like Nichū, aspire to the higher level of education. Unlike the former *kōtō shōgakkō* pupils, the largest number of the new system's middle school pupils are motivated to academic study that will prepare them for successful entrance to secondary education channels. Postwar high schools have expanded their openings far beyond those provided for prewar *chūgakkō* schooling, but the demand for admittance to secondary education is still greater than can be accommodated in the public high schools open to Nichū graduates.

Having located Nichū School within its community and school system settings, we can now look at its internal structure and culture. In the same way that anthropologists describe the social structure, mores, and rituals of isolated social groups, we will describe similar features of the Nichū School's social system.

3 / Nichū

INITIATION

THE TRANSITION from elementary school *jidō* (child, pupil) to middle school *seito* (pupil, student) for the twelve-year-old children of Nichū District involves a distinct change of status in their community. Two ceremonies, about two weeks apart, are dramatic verifications of the change. Graduation from elementary school occurs in the latter part of March. Entrance to middle school follows about two weeks later, with an initiation ceremony for all the new pupils and their parents. Coincident with the short blossoming season of the ornamental Japanese cherry trees, the initiation ceremony cannot escape an inevitable metaphor in Japanese thinking. The blossoms signify a new unfolding and rejuvenation.

Outward symbols of the child's change in status are school clothing and forms of adult name usage. A new uniform is worn because the Nichū school requires it. Most of the children wear uniforms to the elementary school in the upper grades, but they are not required by the school. The middle school uniform is of a different design and the brass buttons are embossed with the Chinese characters for "Nichū." Boys wear black trousers and high-collared coats with attached celluloid collars. Girls wear sailor suits of navy blue. The ostensible purpose of the prescribed uniform is to eliminate socioeconomic distinctions among students that would be made explicit in the clothes worn to school. That parents insist on school uniforms is the common reason that teachers give for their required usage. There is no national policy to either promote or discourage the use of uniforms.

The second symbol of the child's change in status is the more formal name usage in the middle school. Middle school teachers will not follow the elementary school practice of calling the children by their first names with the friendly but juvenile "chan" suffix. Signifying the advance to adolescent status, the students will be called by their last names. Boys have *kun* appended to their names (a form of "Mr." used for inferiors or friends) and girls will have *san* added to theirs (Mr. Mrs., and Miss—used for any situation and not implying either inferior or friendly connections.)

Entrance to a school in Japan, at any level, calls for a special ceremony or initiation conducted in a formal manner. Entrance to elementary school is, for Nichū parents and children, the first such ceremony, except for those who have attended the kindergarten ceremony. No less important is the middle school initiation—the last initiation ceremony in which the children of the community will participate with all of their agemate neighbors.

29

Three times during the school year, the Nichū principal puts on his formal suit of striped trousers and tails. The initiation ceremony for first year middle school pupils (seventh graders) is the first such occasion. (New Year's Day assembly and graduation are the only other school ceremonies that demand this degree of formality.) Appropriate to the gravity of the initiation ceremony is the presence of the PTA chairman, PTA officials, and the two elementary school principals from the Nichū District. Parents and relatives attend, but second and third-year pupils do not. For the ceremony, parents (for the most part, mothers) dress in their best kimonos. (At ordinary school meetings, parents usually wear the more casual, Western-style dress.) The children are all well scrubbed. Most of the boys have close-cropped haircuts. The brand new uniforms, to be worn everyday for a variety of school activities, will rarely look so clean again. Only a few threadbare suits, inheritances from an older brother or sister, are in evidence.

In front of the school, children and parents gather while they find their class assignments in lists posted on the outside bulletin board. Special visitors go on to the principal's office and sip a cup of tea. Though conversation is cordial in the office, arrival of the Nichū PTA chairman changes the atmosphere and conversation becomes centered on him. He is obviously the man to whom others defer, including the three school principals.

Meanwhile, the middle school teachers busily organize the children into class groups for the march into the assembly hall. The ceremony is held in three classrooms that feature removable partitions. Desks have been moved out. Additional chairs have been brought in.

Children are marched into the hall and seated in class groups. Boys sit on one side of the hall, girls on the other. (Separation of the sexes is a ceremonial pattern; in ordinary classroom activities boys and girls will sit in systematically integrated patterns.) Behind the children and along one side of the long hall, seats are placed for the parents. In front, there is a raised platform, a speaker's lectern, and a large Japanese flag, flanked by velvet curtains, tacked to the wall and extending from ceiling to floor. A big vase of flowers on a small table is the other ceremonial symbol, together with the flag. Teachers sit on one side at the front of the hall. Visitors and officials are guided in last to sit across from the teachers.

While the principal stands behind the lectern facing the children, the head teacher calls the roll of new pupils. Each answers his name with a loud and quick *hai* (yes).

In the fashion of a military drillmaster, the physical education teacher gives rapid-fire loudspeaker commands to the children to stand and bow before and after each of the ceremonial speeches by the principal, an elementary school principal, and the PTA chairman.

The speeches take the form of ceremonial, moral exhortations. The principal tells the children of the kindness and zeal of their teachers and the PTA officials. One example of PTA enthusiasm he mentions is the new school gymnasium that will be built during the year, financed in large part by the PTA chairman's personal donation of money. When finished, it will be one of the outstanding school buildings of the prefecture.

Nichū calligraphy class. Notice that each pupil wears a name tag.

Mention of the new gymnasium leads into an explanation of the school motto which has been painted in traditional calligraphy on a large sheet of paper and fastened to the curtain behind the speaker's platform. The principal explains the three-word motto: *jishu* (independence, autonomy) means that the pupil must be independently able to judge between right and wrong; *kinro* (labor, diligence, personal service) means that the pupil must work hard at all his activities including both study and sports; *kyōei* (mutual prosperity) comes from cooperation with one's classmates.

Then the PTA chairman speaks, with a thick dialect in the local vernacular. He is seriously intent as he shouts at the children in front of him, disregarding the microphone that is amplifying his already overly-loud voice. By contrast with the principal's cultured speech, the PTA chairman conveys little of meaning to the American observer. The manner of interaction and attitude conveyed in both his ceremonial speech and in his other PTA activities seem to indicate that he enjoys the prestige accorded his position. Though a man of little education, his business acumen and affluence have allowed him to become a *yūryokusha* (man of importance) in the community. His PTA position is a public affirmation of his locally achieved status. He feels like a *sensei* (teacher) and afterwards describes his position in this manner directly to the author. For thirteen years he has "served" as Nichū PTA chairman, only three of which coincided with his only son's middle school education. He chose the site on which the school was to be built, supervised its construction, and is now the contractor for the new gym. "We all like glory, but the chairman likes it more than most people," remarked another PTA official privately.

When a pupil representative comes forward to speak on behalf of the entering class, the microphone is moved from the raised platform to the floor, emphasizing the lower status of the pupil. After bowing to the official visitors, the boy recites quickly a memorized paragraph in a monotone, and returns to his place with the rest of the pupils. Less formally, the principal comes forward to introduce the teachers to the pupils. As each class stands, in turn, the appropriate home room teacher is introduced. The teacher and his class exchange formal bows after the principal's introduction. He introduces the rest of the teachers quickly, and mentions the subjects they teach. Then the head teacher steps forward to pronounce the ceremony closed.

Nichū teachers at work in the teachers' room after school.

Ceremonial activities over, the official visitors retire to the principal's office for lunch. The children and their parents go to the classrooms to meet the home room teachers. The rest of the teachers retire to the teachers' room where they have their twenty-five desks arranged together in four rows. Since most teachers do not have regularly assigned classrooms, they are expected to go to the pupils' home rooms for instruction. Subjects requiring special equipment are the exception. The teachers' room is the center of staff activity between classes, during free periods, and before and after school.

The final activity of initiation is the collection of the PTA initiation fee of 200 yen ($.56) from each parent, money that will be used for regular school expenses.

Thus the child is initiated into a school program that will mark a time of cultural compression.* The elementary school, perhaps more easygoing in its postwar

---

* "Cultural compression" occurs when demands on children by cultural transmitters (teachers, parents, etc.) to observe cultural norms are intensified, and the range of tolerated behaviors become narrower (compare Spindler 1960:38–43).

than prewar version, is followed by the middle school where children must now actively begin preparation to qualify for the future role they desire. For most children, it is a time of intensive academic study that will lead inexorably up to the entrance examinations for public high school at the end of their third-year course. The transition to intensive academic study will not be as sudden as the entrance into middle school, but the compressive pressures will gradually be increased in the three-year period. The most severe compression will come to those children with the greatest ambition, those who aspire to an Ichikō education that will lead on to the even more severe university entrance examinations.

The ceremonies of elementary school graduation and middle school initiation mark the outward status changes of the children in their community. The scholastic pressures upon the children, however, have been gradually building up—reinforced by home, community, and school. The teachers gradually apply more and more pressures for academic endeavor as the children advance through the elementary school. The ceremonial break is an affirmation by school and community of the additional responsibility and effort that will be expected of all adolescents.

CLASSROOM ORGANIZATION

The Nichū pupil comes to school six days a week. The school's daily schedule is changed slightly, depending on the season, since there is no daylight saving time in Japan and there is no heating system for the classrooms in winter. In the summer, children are in school for about seven and a half hours a day; in the winter for about six and a half hours. Most third-year pupils add an extra one and a half hours daily, except Saturday, through participation in the late-afternoon voluntary review classes (*kagai*) which are considered essential preparation for the high school entrance examinations. There are six academic class periods a day with four on Saturday. Winter classes are for forty-five-minute periods, summer classes are extended to fifty-minute periods. At the beginning and end of the day there is a short home room period. Twenty minutes a day is set aside for cleaning up this school where no janitors or maintenance personnel are employed.

Essentially, the program of study at Nichū is a one-track curriculum with some separation of pupils into groups according to their post-graduation plans. Such separation does not occur until the second year, when pupils with no further academic ambition elect the vocational education courses over English. The remaining pupils are grouped by ability for the English period in their second and third years of study. During the third year, one additional elective is open to them. Of this non-vocational group, the pupils desiring to go on to high school take a supplementary mathematics course, while those lacking that desire take an additional hour a week each of art and music. Subjects studied by the pupils at Nichū are given in Table 4.

Though the teacher-pupil ratio is 1:36, class groups are considerably larger and teachers are allowed one or more free periods a day. The average home room class has forty-eight pupils. Table 5 shows the number of classes and pupils in Nichū.

TABLE 4

REQUIRED AND ELECTIVE COURSES OFFERED AT NICHŪ

Class	Required or Elective	Number of Class Meetings Per Week		
		Seventh Grade	Eighth Grade	Ninth Grade
Japanese Language	Required	5	4	5
Social Studies	"	4	5	4
Mathematics	"	4	4	3
Science	"	4	4	4
Music	"	2	2	1
Art	"	2	2	1
Health and Physical Education	"	3	3	3
Vocational Education and Home Economics	"	3	3	3
English	Elective	4	4	5
Industrial Education	"	–	4	5
Supplementary Home Economics	"	–	4	5
Supplementary Math	"	–	–	2
Supplementary Music	"	–	–	1
Supplementary Art	"	–	–	1
Moral Education	Required[a]	2	2	2
Home Room and Club Activities	Required[b]	1	1	1
Total Class Hours Per Pupil		34	34	34

[a] Not classified as an academic course, but a required course in the national curriculum.
[b] Required activities in the school program, but not academic courses.

Responsibility for the school program rests with the principal and twenty-three teachers of whom eighteen are male and five are female.

Classroom instruction and pupil participation in the classroom activities follow certain forms and patterns. Though individual teachers use a variety of different teaching techniques and exhibit a variety of different behavior patterns before the pupils, there are certain fixed physical and social arrangements that are followed by all.

In the classroom's physical arrangements and the standardized, polite forms of behavior expected of pupils, emphasis is placed on respect for the teacher who holds the time-honored Japanese title of *sensei*. The literal meaning of *sensei* is "teacher" and the word is used both as a noun and as an honorific form of address for respected elders, medical doctors, priests, professors, private tutors in tradition-al arts, and school teachers. It replaces the *san* suffix (Mr. Mrs., or Miss) used with the last names of such people. Nichū teachers, referring to themselves in front of

TABLE 5

NICHŪ PUPILS

Year	Home Room Class Groups	Male	Female	Total	Average Class Size
First	5	115	122	237	47
Second	6	157	130	287	48
Third	6	135	162	297	50
Total	17	407	414	821	48

their pupils, will also use *sensei* as a first person personal pronoun. For example, "That's a difficult point. *Sensei* will explain it." Similarly, teachers speaking about or calling to another teacher will use it as a second or third person personal pronoun, as long as they are in school. Outside the school, pupils will not change in their usage of this respect form, but teachers may switch to a more intimate personal pronoun when referring to fellow teachers.

A long history of respect for the *sensei* in Japanese society has helped to keep the public status of teachers at a high level. Indicative of this status is the high percentage of Japanese men who become teachers. Teaching has never been considered a feminine occupation in a nation where masculine identification is an important element of professional status. Though women have broken into the teaching ranks throughout the last century, the result has not, apparently, been a feminization of the teaching role. In 1960, 55 percent of Japanese elementary school teachers, 78 percent of middle school teachers, and 81 percent of high school teachers were men (Japan, Office of the Prime Minister 1962:459–61).

Nichū classrooms are physically arranged to emphasize the difference in teacher and student levels. At the front of each classroom there is a raised platform on which stands a desk or lectern for the teacher's notes and books while he is lecturing. Pupils sit at rough wooden desks with separate simple wood chairs. Most of the furniture is undersized for children today whose height and weight is greater than that of previous generations. In usual practice, the desks are arranged in rows, with boys and girls systematically seated in alternate seats. Only one Nichū class separate boys and girls on opposite sides of the classroom.

Ideal standards of classroom behavior demand that all pupils be in the classroom before the teacher arrives; stand up quickly at his entry; bow at a signal from the teacher or a pupil officer before taking their seats; stand up beside their desks when spoken to, called upon, or for recitation; sit quietly with rigid posture between such interludes; and at the close of the class stand and bow to the teacher. In practice, these forms are enforced by some teachers who will often interrupt their lectures to remind pupils of proper practice. Some teachers can get the correct responses automatically from their pupils; most have to give direct reminders. Female teachers and younger male teachers, however, often have difficulty maintaining a semblance of "proper" order. Older, more severe teachers, with experience that dates to the prewar and wartime periods when behavior and discipline received more emphasis, often emphasize matters of classroom behavior.

One of the old-timers in teaching is Tanaka-sensei, who has a military bearing and an air of authority used in enforcing classroom order. Entering the classroom after the ten-minute break between classes, he witnesses the usual confusion among the children. Not supervised during the break periods, the children move freely in and out of the classroom, engaging in a good deal of horseplay. This is their time to relax and teachers are loathe to interfere with it.

Tanaka-sensei goes immediately to the front of the room and stands on the same level as the children and draws his stomach in to assume the military drill posture of "attention." As the children notice him, they become quiet and warn their classmates of his presence. He waits stiffly for several moments, but will call out sharply, "You're slow, you're slow," if the children do not calm down and stand beside their desks. Then he bows deliberately. The children respond by performing their bows and sitting down at their desks without a further sign from him.

On one occasion, he reproved his class for misbehavior by saying, "We are not learning *only* social studies here."

The pupils' major activities center around listening and note-taking. As the teacher lectures, he pursues the standard practice of outlining on the blackboard the points which he considers important. These may be taken directly from the teachers' manual for each textbook, which usually carries a column of such points at the top of each page, or they may be original with the teacher. Pupils are expected to copy in their notebooks all the notes written by the teacher on the blackboard.

Encouragement is sometimes given to the pupil to take notes (*memo*) independently on what is being explained, but the outlines on the board (*notto*) are supposed to be copied with neatness and precision. Teachers will often walk about the class to check on pupils' note-taking and will pause in their lecture while the children catch up. Pupil's questions and classroom discussion are rare. Most of the children seem to be unwilling to ask questions or discuss various points, despite overt encouragement from the teacher.

In general, the textbook is the center of classroom instruction. Most classes observed included long periods of direct reading aloud from the textbook. Teachers followed suggestions and outlines given in the teachers' manuals and rarely deviated from the textbook's presentation.

The morals education hour caused teachers special difficulty. Each teacher is expected to give his home room class one hour of this subject each week. There is no textbook for this subject. Teachers are expected to plan and carry out activities based on a general outline but adapted to the circumstances of the community and the school. In practice, the teachers did use one copy of a nonofficial morals education text and teachers' guide. One older teacher consistently carried out his morals education class by giving his sample textbook to one of his pupils who would read from it for about twenty minutes. Then the teacher would read the same selection to his pupils, filling up the rest of the period with his personal comments. A severe teacher, he seemed to scare the children into submission, but an observer at the back of the room could see that some children were covertly doing their mathematics homework whenever they were able to disguise this endeavor from the teacher.

A common pattern in the teaching of morals education was the use of tape-recorded radio programs, taken from the national educational broadcasts, that were designed specifically for classroom use. Such recordings generated a good deal of interest among pupils in particular topics, and would be used to begin a class discussion. Another technique used by Nichū teachers was to have children write anonymous themes on a given topic and use their thoughts as a starting point for comparison and general discussion. Since the themes were anonymous and there were no textbooks associated with the morals education course, the children did not display much interest in it and were lax about handing in their assigned work.

When children are unable to answer a specific question posed by the teacher during recitation, a standard punishment is for the pupils to stand beside their desks until they are called upon again and can answer another question correctly. This is often combined with a systematic recitation in which the teacher calls on pupils in rotation according to the class seating pattern. A female music teacher left children standing when they could not identify certain notes on a musical scale written on the blackboard. One boy was called on four times before he was finally able to arrive at a correct answer—by chance. He was left standing for most of the class period, much to the amusement of his classmates.

Not all teachers are so severe. There are several teachers who attempt to conduct open discussions with their pupils, urging individual expression of ideas and opinions. While following the same formal patterns of class respect, many of the less severe teachers are able to establish some degree of friendly rapport with their pupils in the classroom.

One of the older teachers with extensive prewar teaching experience was able to draw the children into extensive discussions and, at the same time, tolerate noisy side conversation to a degree which would have unnerved most American teachers. He made a point of assigning classroom activities that would allow him time to walk around the classroom and give individual help where it was needed. In his classroom teaching, the author never observed this teacher speaking or acting in a severe manner with the children.

Once, though, when a boy had done something that had upset the teacher, he called him into the teachers' room and lost his temper. He shouted, "Fool," and slapped him twice in the face. The boy stood with his head bowed while the teacher, sitting at his desk, berated him for about five minutes before dismissing him.

The teachers' room was often the site of disciplinary actions. Some teachers would make the offending pupils stand or kneel in the room for periods of time, while others would be dismissed with a severe verbal reprimand. The author observed only two instances of physical punishment in the school during the period of this study.

GUIDANCE AND EXAMINATIONS

One of the major activities of a middle school in Japan is the furnishing of guidance that will enable the child and his family to choose his post-middle school career. By far the largest part of this guidance is involved with the problems of going on to further schooling. Special attention is also given to the smaller group of children who will be seeking jobs directly after middle school graduation.

From the first year of classes in middle school, the teachers begin to talk about the different vocational and educational tracks that will be open to children. In the second year, a choice must be made between the elective courses in English and vocational education. The former is preparation for high school entrance; the latter means the child will not even attempt to enter a public high school. In the third year, the most excruciating choices must be made about which high school to apply to or where to find work. The Nichū school carries a heavy responsibility for assisting the children in their choices.

For the children who decide to try for further education, an intensive program of preparation begins in the second year of their middle school career. They begin to take a series of examinations designed to test their academic achievement in the same manner as the high school entrance examination. The tests used for this purpose at Nichū originate from two prefectural organizations, one a newspaper publishing company and the other a cram school (*yobikō*) for college entrance preparation. The tests are printed and distributed about the prefecture at the same time to the participating middle schools. Only those children who intend to go on to high school take the tests. After being corrected at the individual schools, the test scores are correlated for the prefecture by the organizations concerned so that teachers and children can see how each individual compares with the prefectural norms and distribution. The testing organizations are operated as private businesses and have no connection with the prefectural education office which is responsible for the construction and administration of the actual high school entrance examination.

At the beginning of their third year in the middle school, pupils who intend to go on to high school are counseled by the teachers on the basis of their achievement test scores during the second year. The special tests have two major functions: (1) to give information about the relative academic rank of the pupil for determining to which high school he might have a chance of being admitted and (2) to give the pupils practice in taking such examinations. Test-taking skills are deliberately developed by the Nichū teachers in their administration of the tests. During their third year the pupils take eight of these practice examinations.

To further prepare the third-year pupils for the entrance examination ordeal, *kagai* (extracurricular) review courses are held every afternoon after school and during the summer vacation. Attendance is voluntary but usually includes all children who have any intention of taking the high school entrance examinations as well as a few others who view the course as worthwhile even though they do not plan to take the examinations.

A series of textbooks in each of the examination review subjects is assigned for the pupil participating in the *kagai* classes. They are a special series issued by one of the textbook publishing companies and edited by a prestigious professor of education. The contents include outlines of middle school subject matter and many practice questions on each section. The *kagai* classes center on consideration of these texts with the teachers covering two subjects each day.

In the *kagai* classes, Nichū teachers administer their own examinations about every two weeks and the results are recorded publicly to show the relative standing of the Nichū pupils. Combined with the formal practice tests, the regular school mid-term and term examinations, and the Ministry of Education's nationwide achievement test, the third-year students do not lack an opportunity to practice their test-taking skills.

During the academic year of this study, third-year Nichū pupils intending to enter high school took twenty-seven tests. Mid-term and term examinations accounted for six of these tests; practice entrance examinations from prefectural organizations numbered eight; eleven were given by teachers in their afternoon *kagai* review classes; one was the two-day nationwide achievement test from the Ministry of Education; and the last was the actual prefectural high school entrance examination.

Not only are the pupils involved in examination-preparation activities, Nichū teachers, too, must be prepared to advise their pupils. There are no formal channels of information about relative difficulty of high school entrance requirements and teachers must develop their own sources of information. Information about the relative level of each high school, expressed in the minimum number of points required on the prefectural entrance examination for admission the previous year, is available from the school records. Each year the school is notified of the performance of its pupils on the examinations. The admittances and rejections for each school show where the line was drawn. Even more precise information is obtained by an informal pooling of such data by the five Nippon City middle schools.

Each year, however, new considerations have to be added to the information of previous years. The addition of new classes in a high school means that more children will be admitted. The presence of a larger number of high school applicants means that admission will be more difficult for all schools. To gather more precise information for the purpose of giving individual guidance to pupils in the selection of a high school, Nippon City middle school teacher-representatives meet informally at the end of January to compare notes on the number of high school applicants, the schools they wish to attend, and, most importantly, their performance on the last prefecture-wide practice entrance examination. At this meeting, the teachers can obtain the information they need about chances for entrance to each of the schools.

One teacher described to the author privately an important qualification in the working of this system for the exchange of information. One school can gain an advantage for its pupils by deliberately giving out misinformation in this meeting. They can claim to have a large number of applicants for the top high schools with higher practice examination scores than were actually achieved by their pupils. This will give the other schools the impression that their own borderline pupils will have difficulty in admission and may cause them to counsel pupils to apply for a lower-ranking school. Thus, the borderline pupils of the first school will face less competition in their application for admission to the higher-ranking school.

Since the fate of individuals and the reputation of the school hangs on admission to the top-level high schools, it is possible that teachers could occasionally feed false information into the informal data-gathering system. The refusal of the prefectural education office to acknowledge or make public the real academic-level differences between high schools allows the system described above to continue.

Though public concern has been expressed in the popular press about the antisocial effects of high school entrance examination pressures upon children, the author has seen no reference to the problems of teachers in this situation.

One might note here that the teachers' role, both formally and informally, is always a supportive one with respect to the children. Once admitted to the middle school the child's graduation is assured as long as he comes to school. The teachers have no authority over him with respect to admission to higher levels of education. The admissions process is entirely out of their hands. All they can do is to help the children prepare to meet the impersonal forces and requirements for high school admission. Success in the examinations is the goal of both pupil and teacher. Nothing in the system gives the teacher the additional responsibility of deciding whether or not a child will be recommended for high school entrance. Nor has the teacher had any part in setting the requirements. His only job is to evaluate the pupil's chances of passing the examinations for high school admittance.

The Nichū school has a well-organized system of guidance for those children who will not be continuing their education after middle school graduation. Unlike the pressures that surround high school admittance, finding a job is far less an ordeal. More job openings exist than there are middle school graduates to fill them.

Funneling children into appropriate jobs is a responsibility which the teachers share with the local employment office of the Ministry of Labor. Each year one of the Nichū teachers is assigned the responsibility for liaison with that office and for general guidance of those pupils looking for work. Such children are not necessarily relieved from examination pressure. The larger firms often use examinations, too, in their selection of employees.

The largest group of graduates going to work finds employment in Tokyo. Often, the teacher responsible for this guidance will make arrangements to take the pupils to Tokyo to give them an opportunity to visit the sites of possible jobs.

The Nichū school accepts much responsibility for channeling the child into his future. Educational goals are seen as instrumental to the achievement of social and economic positions in the society for the child and the school's organization reflects this position.

PUPIL ORGANIZATION AND SELF-GOVERNMENT

An elaborate structure for self-government and responsibility is a regular part of the Nichū activities for pupils. All pupils are members of two formal groups. Most important is the home room, which is the basic class organization of the school. Once a week, each class holds a home room business session supervised by the home room teacher. Elected class officers preside at these meetings.

In addition, the pupils are assigned to *buraku* residential groups. *Buraku* group meetings are held about once a month and have the major purpose of planning local *buraku* pupil activities, particularly those that will be held during the summer or winter vacation periods. One teacher is assigned to each *buraku* group as an adviser.

On a more selective basis, there are a number of committees (*bu*) set up to carry out specific items of school business. They are composed of representatives from each home room, with one boy and one girl elected to serve on each committee. Twelve of these committees include: school activities (*seikatsu bu*), statistical, library, audiovisual equipment, health, sports, public welfare (*kōsei bu*) which is responsible for the school store, school repairs, newspapers, bulletin board, finance, and school lunch.

The school council or central committee (*chūō iinkai*) is then composed of elected representatives from each *buraku* group and each committee, but not from the home rooms. The school council is responsible for the indirect election of a school president (*seitochō*).

Though few major purposes are served by most of these groups, except the home rooms, the organization is maintained and elections for each official position are held three times a year. Regular *buraku* group and committee meetings are scheduled once a month. Each *buraku* group meets at the same hour and each committee meets at a separate specified time.

The school council and the school activities committee are interdependent in their organization. The activities committee meeting always precedes the council meeting and is responsible for suggesting monthly slogans to the council, which then chooses one for specific enforcement during the coming month. Teacher-advisers participate actively in this process.

At one meeting, the following slogans were suggested by the activities committee:

1. Keep our uniforms in good order.
2. Strive to settle down in our learning.
3. Let us use proper etiquette.
4. Let us keep our bodies' environment clean.
5. Let us be quiet in our classrooms.
6. Let us settle down to business in our activities (*seikatsu*).
7. Let us preserve public morals, such as not entering rooms with our shoes on.

In the next hour, the school council met, elected its officers, and chose one of the slogans for emphasis in the coming month. It was then written on every home room blackboard and the pupils and teachers were expected to enforce the rule. Throughout all the school council activities observed by the author, the pupils were led and dominated by the teachers. However, the pupils did lead one revolt.

During the December meetings of the school activities committee and the school council, the teacher-advisers asked the pupil representatives to approve a list of rules entitled "Proper Living for Winter Vacation." The rules specified in great detail many kinds of behavior expected of children during their winter vacation from school. Few of the rules had any explicit connection with school or academic responsibilities.

The list of rules which the teachers had written and presented to the pupils in duplicated form listed the school council and the school activities committee as the source of the rules. Much to the surprise of the teachers, two of the third-year boys on the school council, one the son of the local newspaper publisher, decided to openly criticize the rules they had been asked to approve. Instead of approving the rules, the council exceeded its alloted time by several hours in a discussion of the specific rules and ended without giving them general approval.

The teacher-advisers were taken aback by the pupil revolt, shocked that the children did not easily accept the rules that they had prepared in the usually accepted form and procedure. One of the younger teachers, who described the revolt to the author, mused, "It would have been better if the pupils had written the rules. Then it would have been easier to get their approval."

One of the rules specified that the children could go only to those movies approved by the school or to those where they were accompanied by their parents. The teachers were worried about the bad influences of the movie theater, "a place where delinquents congregate and smoke in the dark." But the pupils leading the council revolt wanted to be able to go to the movies with their friends and did not agree to the rule. They questioned other rules which specified that they should wear their school uniforms when going to town and that they should not carry pocket knives.

While they were being critical, the pupils brought up a second, unrelated issue. Disapproving of the indirect election of a school president by the council, they asked for direct elections by the school. One of the teachers indicated that such a change had been discussed and might be made in the following year. The third-year pupils were not satisfied with this answer because they wanted to participate in such an election, but would be graduated before the system could be changed.

Conscious of his father's position in the community and secure in his own status as an able pupil, the newspaper publisher's son led the critical revolt. After three hours of discussion, with no decision reached, the council called a special meeting for further consideration of the rules. In the following meeting, the rules were approved as originally stated and distributed to the children and parents. Still, the council and the third-year pupils had had their day of revolt.

The revolt was interesting in view of the local community feeling that Nichū pupils were especially meek and mild in comparison with other middle school districts in Nippon City.

In spite of a textbook and teacher-centered school curriculum, however, Nichū pupils are not necessarily ready to accept without question the guidance of their teachers. Individualistic self-concerns are expressed in certain situations.

Having completed the description of the school and its setting within the local community and formal educational structure, we can now turn to the dynamic interplay of the school with its environment. The preceptions of educational goals within the local community and the range of variation in school experiences in different sections of that community will be taken up in the next chapter.

4 / The local community and the school

I N ORDER TO ASCERTAIN the views of the local community with respect to the school, the author conducted an interview survey of the parents of fifty-three third-year Nichū pupils. Since the interview included open-ended questions, responses were not always directly comparable, but were indicative of personal interests related to the school. General themes that emerged from analysis of the interviews were:

1. There should be a stronger morals education program in the school.

2. Achievement within the school's academic program is the most important concern of parents, with respect to their children. Achievement, in this sense, means the children's ability to pass the entrance examination for high school rather than their ability as measured by grades shown on report cards.

Though specific questions about morals education were reserved until the last part of the interview, prior questions, particularly about a comparison of prewar and postwar patterns of Japanese education, brought comments about the need for strengthened morals education from sixteen of the fifty-three families interviewed. Half of this group was concerned with the problem of getting children to show proper respect for their elders and superiors (*meue*). Including respondents who did not indicate their interest in morals education until asked directly, forty-three families showed interest in strengthening one or more aspects of the *dōtoku* (morals education) course. Twenty-three people related the question about morals education (*dōtoku*) to their own prewar moral education (*shūshin*). Eleven respondents emphasized the similarity between prewar and postwar morals education courses in the school, while twelve emphasized the difference in content. Though direct questions about prewar morals education (*shūshin*) were not a part of the interview schedule, nine people indicated that they would like to have the schools teach a similar course again.

The prewar morals education course (*shūshin*) was abolished by order of the American Occupation, but it was reinstated as *dōtoku* in 1958 by order of the Ministry of Education over the opposition of many groups including the Japan Teachers Union (JTU). The parents of children in the Nichū district were not really aware of what the school was doing for morals education, but they did feel rather strongly that the school should be doing more. Table 6 gives the parents' responses to specific suggestions concerning possible areas for emphasizing *dōtoku* education.

43

TABLE 6

WHAT ASPECTS OF DŌTOKU SHOULD BE STRENGTHENED?

	Agree	Disagree
1. To have regard for (*daiji ni suru*) one's parents.	27	2
2. To have patriotism and love of country (*aikokushin*).	20	4
3. To respect one's superiors (*meue*).	30	—
4. To insist above all on what one believes is right.	19	—
5. Most important is to think of other people more than onself.	8	5

Answers 1, 2, and 3 in Table 6 represent emphases of the prewar *shūshin* course. Number 4 represents an emphasis on individualism. Number 5, which got the least agreement and greatest disagreement, is one way of expressing concern for other people, a rather traditional element of Japanese moralistic thinking. The answers given suggest that the traditional concepts of family and social hierarchy, implied by respect for one's betters, are still strong elements of local thinking. Many of the respondents who did not indicate an interest in morals education were housewives who played the traditional role of the shy and humble Japanese woman. Lack of response in these cases was more indicative of their response to an interview with the strange American. There was no expressed opposition to the idea that the school was responsible for the moral education of children. A few respondents suggested that the family and home had responsibility for moral education also, but this seemed to be, in part, a reflection of views from a recent and prestigious PTA speaker who had emphasized family responsibility in this area.

In addition to specific interview suggestions for strengthening morals education, a number of parents expressed concern over the problems of parent-child relationships and the continuation of the family line. In prewar *shūshin* instruction, the Japanese were made very conscious of their unique family system and the responsibilities of children to their parents and families (Dore 1958:91). Stress was laid on the responsibility of the eldest son to continue the family line, or the eldest daughter if there was no son. The family system was related to the teaching of patriotism in the idea that parent-child and emperor-subject relationships were identical. The Japanese family was "the embodiment of all that was fine and noble in the national tradition, the only suitable training ground for patriotic and loyal citizens, the secret of the moral fibre of the Japanese people, the core . . . of the national polity" (Dore 1958:91).

Thus it was not surprising to find some parents responding to the author's questions about morals education with the idea that patriotism and family obligations were integrally related and could not be taught separately. Fourteen respondents made some specific reference to their desire for moral education related to the family system and children's obligation to their parents, beyond simple choice of the first answer in Table 6.

Quite a few commented that their children were much more impressed by what was said by their teachers than by their parents. Teachers were viewed as having a large influence on the children; thus parents hoped to have the teachers use their prestige with the children to have the children pay attention to their parents. "Rather than teach them to have respect for their parents, just teach them to pay attention to what their parents say," said one mother.

Several farmer-fathers talked at length about the problems involved in guaranteeing that their sons, or, in one case, an eldest daughter, would stay on the farm and continue the family line. In one of the more remote farm *buraku* of Uena Region, a father spoke about the way that few children in the community were really attracted to a farming life. Work in the city seemed much more glamorous and easy. Though his eldest daughter had expressed no desire to leave the family farm, he was still afraid that she might be swayed by the general opinion of her friends and classmates. Lacking sons, he was planning to adopt a husband for her who would be the inheritor of the family farm and the family line.

On the other hand, the mother of another student was very much concerned that her daughter break away from the pattern of the mother's life. Married to a white collar worker, she had to tend the family farm, "My Daughter is too frail for this back-breaking work. She should become an English typist, get a job in the city, and marry into a family where she won't have to farm."

One farm family was disturbed that their eldest son wanted to attend the Kōkō Industrial High School rather than the Rokkō Agricultural High School. The father, badly crippled from World War II and unable to do any farm work, felt that his son should help his mother in the farming rather than planning on a local industrial job toward which the Kōkō course would lead. The deciding factor, in this case, was the boy's lack of ability in achievement test-taking. Luckily, he applied for and was accepted by the Rokkō School. His final entrance test score was too low to have permitted him entrance to the Kōkō Industrial High School, even if he had applied there.

Several fathers talked at length about their military education and training with a great deal of nostalgia. The sense of mission and discipline that had been instilled was obviously important to these men. They felt that the postwar schools should be teaching and instilling a similar kind of discipline. One mother reminisced about the Japanese spirit (*yamatodamashii*) which had been a part of her education. She related it to her *shūshin* course. "When I was a girl, *shūshin* was the most important to me."

A white-collar commuter who worked in Tokyo indicated his desire for inculcation of a vigorous patriotism and Shinto religious instruction in the schools. "In my time we learned respect for religious observances at school. The children today aren't learning these." Then he demonstrated the worshipful handclapping which is properly performed before a Shinto shrine. At this point, a college-student daughter listening unobserved in the next room, was unable to restrain herself further and came out to remonstrate with her father. "The democratic younger generation thinks just the opposite," she said. But only four of the parents interviewed expressed overt opposition to the suggestion of more emphasis on patriotism in the schools, as shown in Table 6.

In an attempt to sound out parents' opinions about the school's academic subjects, the following question was asked: "What educational content (*kyōiku naiyō*) would you like to have strengthened in the present schools?" Sixteen parents responded with suggestions about morals rather than academic education. Thirteen could give no answer, even after a list of suggestions was read that included, (1) reading and writing, (2) history and geography, (3) scientific knowledge, (4) technical understanding, (5) understanding of labor and occupations, and (6) understanding of government and society. No one picked any of the suggested choices enthusiastically, as they did later with the question about moral education. A few agreed that all the suggestions were possible subjects for greater emphasis in the school, or would name courses in which their own children were receiving poor grades. Eleven parents indicated an interest in stronger English language education. Some did so because they had heard that Nichū was specifically weak in its English teaching. A few others stressed the need for better oral instruction in the language. National Language and the writing of *kanji* (Chinese characters) were suggested by eight parents for more emphasis. These parents were critical of the shortened official list of *kanji* which children now learn in the schools, compared with their own prewar education. Only three parents expressed any desire for more vocationally oriented education. One of these wanted an expanded home economics program, while another parent thought that the home economics program already took up too much time that should be spent on academic matters.

Nine parents replied to the academic content question with a specific statement that they did not feel competent to answer it. "Since I have faith in the teachers, I'll let them decide." "The teachers know better." "Since the times have changed, I don't know." The parents generally felt competent to answer questions about morals instruction, but not about academic instruction.

In commenting about the differences between their own and their children's education, twenty-three parents mentioned specifically that prewar teachers had been fear-inspiring, much stricter, or more severe in their ways than teachers now. Ten referred to instances of physical punishment of prewar pupils. Such observations were generally followed with the suggestion that postwar teachers are more like friends of the children. Seven ventured the opinion that present teachers should be more severe and strict (*kibishii*) in their dealings with the students, though the only question asked was about the observations of differences between prewar and postwar teachers.

Discipline (*shitsuke*) was considered an important component of morals (*dō-toku*) teaching. Though parents approved of, to a degree, friendly relations between teachers and pupils, there was an underlying assumption that teacher friendliness and student discipline were not compatible. Several comments were made that indicated distinctly different perceptions of teacher and parent roles. Parents are not expected to, and do not, severely discipline their own children, but they sometimes expect teachers to perform this function. It is assumed, therefore, that they cannot teach their own children. In traditional crafts like *tatami* mat-making, sons who will succeed their fathers in the business are sent to someone else for apprenticeship in the trade. After they learn the job, they come back home to work with their fathers.

Dore has described the same pattern for sons of prewar landlords who used to be sent as live-in workers to the homes of other landlords as a part of their education. "The theory is that parents are inevitably too lenient to their own children and a period of 'eating someone else's rice' is a necessary means of character training" (1959:32). In one farm household, a younger bachelor brother of the family head, living with the family, worked as a private tutor of middle school and high school students. When the author asked if the middle school student daughter sometimes received tutoring help, the mother said, "Oh no. Since he's a member of the family (*miuchi*) . . ." She did not finish the sentence, but she implied that being a member of the family meant that he could not be a teacher for his niece.

Morality, to the parents, is something that must be inculcated through discipline. Teachers, more than parents, are able to be strict with children and are, therefore, the best agents for moral inculcation. The Japanese family system is bound up in the continuing interdependence of parents and children, so parents must avoid alienation of their children's affection. Nichū parents do not state their case for morals education in the schools in these terms, but the underlying rationale is apparent.

> Parents in large part habitually disavow responsibility for forming the child's viewpoint outside of the home, as is evidenced by their frequent pleas to revive the course on ethics in the schools. Behind their attitude is the view that teachers, like other public officials, are not just ordinary persons subject to human frailties and errors in spite of their training but are members of a superior class who are trusted to live up to the standards which qualify that class for leadership and authority (Beardsley, Hall, and Ward 1959: 308).

This emphasis upon morals education in the school is by no means unique to relatively unsophisticated areas like the Nichū District, still bound by traditional patterns of life. Dore's study of an urban Tokyo ward included an interview questionnaire which asked parents specifically if they thought that prewar ethics courses should be reinstated in the schools. His study was conducted in 1951, before the official reinstatement of morals education. Eighty percent of his urban sample responded with a definite answer that they wanted such instruction in the schools.

> The most frequently expressed reason was that the children are badly 'behaved', 'don't know how to be polite' and 'have no respect for their elders'. The most common theme in justifying the need for an ethics course was that the children are no longer told the stories of famous men to inspire them— the old stories of Ninomiya Sontoku, Benjamin Franklin, Jenner or Noguchi . . . The necessity of teaching children to be filial to their parents is the next most common theme (1958:233).

The story of Ninomiya Sontoku, an early nineteenth century Confucian moralist, was much used in prewar *shūshin* instruction as an exemplary model for children to follow. His statue which shows him as a boy carrying a load of wood on his back and, at the same time, reading a Confucian classic, stood outside many prewar elementary schools.

Symbolic of the school's continuing responsibility for morals education, the statue is still to be found in front of the Uena Elementary School.

Questions about future plans for their children elicited general anxiety from parents with respect to the high school entrance examinations that were only about six months away. Forty of the fifty-three families interviewed were planning to send their children on to high school. A few still had not decided whether to have their children apply for further education. Students who were at the very top of their class academically did not cause concern to their parents, but the majority were close to the borderline of acceptance of one or another of the high schools.

Thirty parents indicated some concern about their children's entrance to high school, usually related to the idea that their children would have to study harder in order to make the necessary score on the prefectural entrance examination for the high school of their choice.

Reports of teacher-parent conferences elicited during the interviews confirmed general observation of teacher-parent conferences at the school and elsewhere. Test results related to expectations for achievement on the high school entrance examination were the main subject discussed when teachers and parents conferred. The middle school is, by reason of its position at the terminus of compulsory education, considered the most powerful agency in the determination of whether a child will be able to go on to secondary education and the kind of education for which he will be able to qualify.

The extent and quality of advanced education which one can acquire after finishing the compulsory phase of schooling is, in turn, the single, most important factor in the type of job and social status to which one can aspire. Nagai Michio, a Japanese sociologist, has observed that inter-generational mobility rather than intra-generational mobility is the characteristic form of social mobility in Japan, and that school education received is the determining factor in Japanese inter-generational mobility. Nichū parents are generally aware of this process. Thus they look to the school, and more directly, to the ninth-grade home room teachers, who have the responsibility for guidance of the children's future, for whatever help or influence they can bestow.

From the parents' point of view, the teacher wields tremendous power over the children's future. The teacher must guide the children into the highest educational path for which they can be expected to qualify. If he misjudges the child's ability to perform on the final entrance examination, the child will be condemned to a lower educational and social position than he might otherwise have attained. If the teacher aims him too high, failure for entrance to a first-rate high school will disqualify the child from the second-rate public high school, as well. If the child applying to a second-rate school does unexpectedly well on the entrance examination, he is still restricted to the second-rate high school, though his examination performance would have been sufficient to admit him to the first-rate high school. In either case, the child loses and is condemned to a lower educational track than his achievement on the tests would have qualified him. In the eyes of the parents, there has been a drastic failure on the part of the teacher, who recommended the wrong path in the first place. The teacher is expected to reliably predict success or failure on the entrance examination.

One urban mother interviewed described how her oldest son, now employed in Tokyo, had been misdirected by his middle school teacher. According to her story, the boy had had his heart set on attending Ichikō High School and the teacher had not indicated any "danger" in this ambition to either the boy or his parents until two hours before the deadline for submitting high school applicat ons. Then the teacher called the boy in and advised him to change his application from Ichikō to Sankō High School, because he was in "danger" of failing the Ichikō examination requirements. The parents were not consulted and the boy was disconsolate. He tried to commit suicide. The parents were still angry that there had been no advance warning of the teacher's shift in opinion about the boy's ability.

Parental concern for their children's future was usually expressed in terms of entrance to the specific advanced educational opportunity which they desired for their children. One ambitious shopkeeper-mother whose boy had only a mediocre school record bemoaned the fact that he would not get into one of the six best universities if he did not manage, somehow, to gain admittance to Ichikō High School.

Another mother, whose son was in the top 5 percent of his class, was greatly concerned already with his eventual possibilities for entering Tokyo University, the most prestigious university of Japan. There was no doubt about her son's ability to pass the Ichikō High School examination, but the visit of an interviewer affiliated with Tokyo University immediately made her anxious to establish whatever connections would be possible. "Tokyo University Sickness" (*Tōdaibyō*) was the diagnosis of the author's assistant as he refused to accept a large and expensive box of grapes which the mother wanted to present to the interviewing team.

Girls' parents talked about educational channels that would be prestigious when their daughters were considered as brides. The girls could be socially mobile through marriage, depending on their educational background.

A policeman's wife was very anxious to get the interviewer's opinion about the relative merits of the night school course at Ichikō High School, compared with the private girls high school in Nippon City. Her daughter would take the entrance examination for Nikō High School, but her grades indicated that this was a "dangerous" course of action. The daughter was, indeed, one of the twenty-one pupils in the interview sample who were eventually unable to enter the high school they desired at the time of the interview. On the other hand, nineteen pupils succeeded in entering the high school chosen at the time of the interviews.

Further indication of anxiety surrounding the preparation for high school entrance examination was the fact that twenty of the forty pupils hoping for a high school education in the interview sample had received special private tutoring in their own homes (*katei kyōshi*) or at local classes (*juku*). Such tutoring was generally carried out several evenings a week and in the summer vacation. This was in addition to the regular review classes given daily after school at Nichū for the third-year pupils planning to take the high school entrance examinations.

Parents' descriptions of the factors that they were considering in choosing a high school showed that they were primarily interested in the social paths that each high school could open up to its students. Of the nine girls in the interview sample who might have qualified academically for Ichikō High School, all were planning to enter Nikō High School. Some wanted to go on to college, but not necessarily to one of the high-prestige universities. Nikō is the channel to a good marriage, but Ichikō leads to the prestige universities and masculine social roles.

Parents were generally concerned that their daughters stay in a feminine school environment, and a number expressed opposition to the idea of coeducational high schools. Two parents indicated they would like their daughters to try for Ichikō High School, but the girls did not want to go there.

Though the information in Chapter 2 about the relative ranking of Nippon City high schools was based on confidential data, the parents interested in sending their children to high school showed a high level of awareness of relative rankings of the different high schools and a good deal of familiarity with the technicalities of the achievement tests that were given regularly to the pupils by the teachers as practice for the entrance examinations. Past test results used by teachers for guidance purposes were well-known by the parents. One farm parent explained the practice tests accurately to the author's interpreter, including the long and involved name of the prefectural organization responsible for constructing the test and the scores required for certain entrance to the local prestige high schools.

A junk dealer, talking of the possibility of his youngest son going on to high school, said, "I'd like at least one of my three sons to rise in society." The high school was the direct and only path for any of his sons to "rise in society." A mother raised on a farm said, "Before the war some children would pursue their studies and others wouldn't. Now, even in the farm homes, the children are told to study. If one doesn't study, he won't rise to distinction." The school as a path for social mobility is recognized as such by parents. Most seem anxious to push their children along this path if the child has the academic ability and the family has sufficient financial resources.

However, not all children and their parents aspire to higher education and the social position that goes with it. Ninety-eight of the 297 children in the Nichū Class of 1963, or 33 percent of the class, had decided by the second term to not attempt to continue their formal education, because of low grades, economic necessity, or lack of desire. These children would remain at home after graduation or go away for jobs. The school, however, is still the responsible agent for channeling them in their future economic and social roles. This is so because the school arranges job placement for these children with the assistance of of the Nippon City Employment Office, an agency of the national government. The ninth-grade home room teachers are given the major responsibility for the guidance involved, and the parents look to them for the help that they can give. "I hope the teacher can find a good job for my boy," said the old woman who acted as her grandson's guardian.

Besides the responsibility which the school holds for guiding the children to their further educational and job channels, it has the basic responsibility for teaching those academic and vocational skills that will be necessary for the next step after middle school. Since 67 percent of the Nichū third-year pupils, would like to continue their education in high school, the most important academic job, perceived by parents and teachers alike, is the preparation that will enable children to do well on their entrance examinations. Schools are publicly evaluated by the percentage of graduates who gain admittance to secondary education. Imparting the skills necessary for test passing is viewed as the teacher's special domain. The parents are mostly convinced that the more hours of instruction that a child can receive and the more hours of independent study that he can put in at home, the better chance he will have to succeed in the all-important examinations. After-school review classes for high school applicants are judged by their length; no mention of the quality or type of instruction is made by the parents. Most parents feel that private tutoring will help their children to better prepare for the tests. "If by going to the private class she can pass her (entrance) tests, then it is good, in spite of the money it will cost."

URBAN-RURAL DIFFERENCES

Few differences were observable between urban Tokai Town and rural Uena Region in the attitudes expressed or implied by the interview sample. There was some difference, however, in the number of children getting private tutoring outside of the school and in the desires for the attainment of prestigeful secondary education.

Table 7 shows that Tokai Town children entered prestige high schools after middle school graduation at a higher rate than the Uena Region children who were more likely to discontinue their education.

TABLE 7

NICHŪ CLASS OF 1963 POSTGRADUATION CAREERS*

	Tokai Town No. Percent		Uena Region No. Percent		Total No. Percent	
1. Prestige high schools (Ichikō, Nikō, and Kōkō)	53	30	14	13	67	24
2. Other public high schools, including night school course	52	30	22	20	74	26
3. Other education (private high schools, etc.)	36	21	24	22	60	21
4. Other (jobs, stay-at-home, etc.)	34	19	49	45	83	29
Total	175	100	109	100	284	100

* Not including 12 orphanage pupils.

Many children from both Tokai Town and Uena Region participate in out-of-school formal education. Table 8 indicates the numbers of children who received some kind of formal instruction outside of the public schools. Children who attended the special private classes in calligraphy (*shūji*) or abacus arithmetic (*soroban*) at any time during their elementary or middle school careers are included in this table. Additionally, any children who received special tutoring at home (*katei kyōshi*) or attended local private classes (*juku*) for help in their middle school studies are listed. Most of the abacus and calligraphy students took their les-

TABLE 8

PARTICIPATION IN FORMAL EDUCATION OUTSIDE OF SCHOOL; NICHŪ CLASS OF 1963*

	Tokai Town			Uena Region			Total Group		
	Boys	Girls	Total	Boys	Girls	Total	Boys	Girls	Total
1. Calligraphy (shūji)	15 18%	38 42%	53 30%	2 4%	21 36%	23 21%	17 12%	59 40%	76 27%
2. Abacus Arithmetic (soroban)	21 25%	44 49%	65 37%	17 33%	25 42%	42 38%	38 28%	69 46%	107 38%
3. Tutoring in Middle School Subjects (juku, katei kyōshi)	29 34%	34 38%	63 36%	13 25%	4 7%	17 15%	42 31%	38 25%	80 28%
Total Number of Children in Class of 1963	85	90	175	51	59	110	136	149	285

* Not including 12 children from the orphanage.

Raising the national flag at the beginning of Nichū's Athletic Day activities.

sons while they were still elementary school pupils. Many children were involved in all three kinds of instruction outside of the public schools.

While basic elements of calligraphy and the abacus are taught in the public schools, the private classes lead to greater proficiency. Calligraphy is taught as a fine art and is considered a desirable accomplishment for young brides, as well as a serious subject for study by both men and women. The abacus instruction is vocationally oriented because it is a required skill for a large number of people employed in commercial activities. Girls outnumber boys in both these types of instruction.

Private classes in calligraphy and abacus arithmetic, observed by the author in a variety of settings, follow in some ways the descriptions available of the premodern *terakoya* schools that used to give commoner children a basic education in reading, writing, and abacus arithmetic. Often taught in one large room to a number of children of all ages, the teacher and student monitors consult with the individual children on their assigned work. Instructional patterns are highly stylized and traditional. The overtones of an abacus instructor's voice reading a problem to his students, like those of an American tobacco auctioneer at work, are easily recognized by one who may not understand a word that is being said.

On the other hand, private tutoring or special classes in middle school subjects are taught in much the same manner as the regular middle school classes. Private teachers are generally university students, "moonlighting" middle school and high school teachers, or retired teachers. A few people make a full-time profession out of such tutoring. The retired principal of another Nippon City middle school put up a special classroom building where his wife teaches sewing classes to girls while he and a staff of part-time college student teach daytime cram school (*yobikō*) courses for middle school *rōnin* (children who failed their high school entrance examinations) and nighttime review classes for middle school pupils preparing for their first high school entrance examinations.

There is little difference between Tokai Town and Uena Region children in their out-of-school participation in the traditionally-oriented abacus and calligraphy classes, but there is a difference in their participation in middle school subject tutoring. Though most of the classes are located in the central part of Nippon City, more easily accessible to the Tokai Town children, the Uena Region children manage to maintain their participation in the traditional classes. But they do not come to town for the middle school tutoring. This is a reflection of their reduced level of interest in going on for further public school education after the middle school. In any case, one may observe again that the two sections of Nichū District are equally traditional in some respects, but the urban Tokai Town residents exhibit greater ambition for their children to gain a high school education.

This difference can be compared with Vogel's observation in a Tokyo middle class community that it is the salary man who must put pressure on his children for academic achievement.

> In planning the future it is the salary man and his family who are most dependent on entrance examinations. Unlike the independent professional or the businessman, who can take the children into his own work regardless of the educational institutions the children attended, and unlike the shopkeeper who has lower aspirations for his children, the salary man's children are dependent upon entrance examinations to universities and companies. Hence, they generally place more pressure on their children and spend more time and energy to prepare them for these examinations (1963:38).

About 70 percent of the people of Uena Region are employed in agriculture, while only about 30 percent are so employed in Tokai Town. The farmer, like the independent professional man in Vogel's study, can usually take at least one son into his own work. Equally important is the fact that farm families tend to have lower aspirations for their children.

Though there is no special difference between boys and girls enrolled in middle school tutoring for the total group studied, there is a major difference between the Uena Region boys and girls who get involved in such out-of-school study. The rural girls of Uena Region are apparently not expected to strive for high school entrance in the same way as the urban girls of Tokai Town. In both regions, however, the girls, much more than the boys, participate in the traditional abacus and calligraphy classes.

Of further interest is a comparison of school achievement within the Nichū school. The middle school grading system is based on a scale of five points with five being the best grade given and one the lowest. These are not interpreted into letter grades or as passing-failing, since no one ever "fails" a course. The poorest student has a 1.0 average and the best a 5.0 average. During 1962, the third-year pupils from Uena Region had a cumulative grade point average of 2.92 while their comrades from Tokai Town had an average of 3.38.

Thus the rural Uena Region children participate equally with the Tokai Town children in traditional out-of-school classes for calligraphy and abacus learning, but they fall behind in middle school tutoring, average school grades, and most importantly, in the proportion of children able to go on to public high schools. Though many more rural families are now seeking further education for their children than before the war, they do not seem to be keeping up with the urban families.

One farm parent in the interview group suggested that farmers are less concerned about education than urban company employees because they always have a source of food and family support. White collar workers do not have security of this sort to pass on to their children, and so must be more concerned to have their children qualify, through education, for the type of job and social position attained by the parents. The same farmer, however, went on to describe his reasons for wishing to enter his daughter in the Nikō High School in terms of the increased advantage she would have for making a good marriage—the form of social mobility open to girls through education.

An additional and important factor in the urban-rural difference, however, is a process of social selection that has been occuring in recent times. Men and women of talent have moved to higher economic and social positions in urban settings through higher educational channels. Those of lesser talents and endowment have been left behind on the farms. Even the emphasis on the eldest son's reponsibility to succeed in the family line has not held back talented eldest sons who have cut their ties with farming or traditional family occupations.

Though attitude differences between Tokai and Uena parents were not apparent in the author's interview survey, it is obvious that educational patterns, participation, and success are substantially different.

The foregoing discussion of community perceptions of the role of the school and differential experiences with the school's program leads naturally to an examination of the forms of social, political, and economic interaction between the school and its community. The following chapter examines specifically both organized and informal forms within which school and community interaction occur.

5 / School and community interaction

ORGANIZATION AND ROLE OF THE PTA

THERE ARE SEVERAL formal organizations associated with Nichū school and its community. Though considered as separate entities, they are, in practice, all part of what is most commonly called the *pīchīē* (PTA). Some activities are labeled as *fukeikai* (parents' association) by the teachers to distinguish meetings called by the school for educational programs aimed at parents, from meetings called to consider the formal business proceedings for the PTA.

A variety of other words also relate to the PTA organization, some of them coming from prewar parents and community organizations designed explicitly to support the school financially. The name *pīchīē* is a postwar introduction, though the organization is similar to prewar school-supporting associations. Separate PTA and *kōenkai* (supporters' association) organizations are maintained by school and community authorities in some parts of Japan. In these cases, the PTA is a parents' organization to facilitate pupil and parent guidance while the *kōenkai* is a community organization specifically designed to collect local "voluntary" financial contributions for school building funds, educational equipment, and operating expenses.

Since the beginning of a modern public school system in Japan, public schools have relied heavily on local fees and "voluntary" contributions to finance a part of the regular school budget, as well as for new buildings and equipment. Because elementary and middle schools are now part of the compulsory education pattern, they both rely on "voluntary" community contributions, much in the form of municipal taxes and often assessed directly on that basis. Local school *kōenkai* in some areas are designed to take care of the financial needs of all public schools, elementary and middle, through one regional organization.

The PTA of Nichū school, however, carries both the *kōenkai* and *pīchīē* functions for the middle school. Informal cooperation with the two elementary school PTA's in the Nichū district serves to apportion and consolidate the different school requests for money, letting the middle school and elementary schools share the available resources. There is no separate *kōenkai* to perform this function. Officers and *buraku-ku* representatives to the different elementary and middle school PTA's are often the same people, so that collections for the two schools will be carried out by the same people at the same time.

Budgets of the municipally-operated elementary and middle schools are the responsibility of the local, city, town, or village assemblies, which finance school expenses through regular municipal taxes. Teachers' and administrators' salaries, however, come directly from the prefecture through the prefectural board of education. They are employees of the prefecture rather than the local board of education. The cost of their salaries is split between the national and prefectural governments. As the major item of school expenditure, exclusion of salaries from the local school's operating budget gives the local school board and school responsibility for only about 35 percent of the money expended on the school's program. There are no direct school taxes in the school district or local community, but the money appropriated by the Nippon City Assembly comes directly from the municipal tax funds. Building of new school facilities is also a responsibility of the local government. In practice, money appropriated by the city is never sufficient for operation of the local schools.

Schools like Nichū must rely upon two further sources of income. First, there is a regular series of monthly fees collected from each pupil, together with special entrance and graduation fees which support, in part, the regular school operating budget. Second, there are community-wide fund drives for special school facilities, not restricted to families with children in school at the time of the collection. The tapping of these two sources of school money is the primary function of the Nichū PTA. Table 9 gives the sources of funds for Nichū in the 1961–1962 school year. Though only 11.3 percent of the total school expenditures came from the local community's donations through the PTA, they were used for the greatest part of the school's operating expenses. In 1961–1962, there was no special drive for community donations. Such drives occur, on the average, every other year. In 1962–1963, there was a general collection for sports equipment to outfit the new gymnasium that was built. At that time, 1,033,430 yen was collected, an average donation of 482 yen per Uena region household and 393 yen per Tokai Town household. At the same time, the PTA chairman personally donated 5 million yen toward the construction of the new gymnasium structure, about 22 percent of the total cost. The rest of the cost was born by a special appropriation and a subsidy from the national government. Thus, though Table 9 shows the city contributing more heavily to capital expenditures than the PTA, a longer-term view would show the PTA contributing about the same amount to the school as the city government.

The regular PTA funds come from the monthly fee of 250 yen collected for each pupil. In addition to community fund drives and student fees, there are other fund-raising activities sponsored by the PTA. One activity is the selling of refreshments to visitors at the annual school athletic meeting (*undōkai*).

Payment of PTA fees and donations is on a voluntary basis and there is no legal means that the school can use to collect them. However, social pressures within the *buraku-ku* sections are strongly oriented toward the fulfillment of such social responsibilities. The Nichū school clerk who handles the bookkeeping suggested that less than one percent of the families give any trouble about paying their children's monthly fees. A few families, in very poor economic circumstances, are informally excused by the teachers from paying the fees and are also helped by donations from PTA funds for children's pocket money on school trips, etc.

The collection of special donations, as those for the new gymnasium equipment

TABLE 9

SOURCES OF NICHŪ SCHOOL FUNDS, 1961-62, IN YEN*

Item	Source of Funds			
	Nation and Prefecture	Nippon City	PTA and Community Donations	Total
1. Teachers' and Principal's pay and allowances	13,231,051 61.1%	—	—	13,231,051 61.1%
2. Operating expenses (incl. pupil welfare services and salaries of non-teaching staff)	61,260 .3%	1,243,111 5.7%	1,973,800 9.1%	3,278,171 15.1%
3. Capital expenditures				
a. New gymnasium	247,500 1.1%	2,552,000 11.8%	—	2,799,500 12.9%
b. Other	202,110 .9%	471,790 2.2%	481,598 2.2%	1,155,498 5.3%
4. Installment on school debt (past school construction)		1,194,064 5.5%	—	1,194,064 5.5%
Total	13,741,921 63.4%	5,460,965 25.2%	2,455,398 11.3%	21,658,284 100.0%

* Taken from Nichū's annual report to the Ministry of Education.

cited above, is carried out by local hamlet representatives (*riji*) of the PTA. In the beginning, a certain goal is set by the PTA organization for each *buraku-ku* group, to apportion the expenses fairly. Then each *buraku-ku* section arranges the way in which it will collect the money to meet its goal. Informally, the amount expected of each household is set and is then tactfully communicated. For larger contributions the amount set is usually based on the amount of taxes paid by the household.

In collecting the donations, one of the *buraku-ku* representatives will visit each household starting with the most prestigious and working his way down the social ladder. Local leaders and political figures are approached first and are expected to make large contributions. The names and the amount contributed by each family are recorded in a book which is shown to each successive donor. The collection involves a formal visit to each household, at which time the prospective donor looks down the list of contributions and makes appropriate exclamations about the generosity of the various donors. He then can figure out for himself, or will be told, the amount expected of his household.

Community cooperation is a strong value in most households and one is usually loath to contribute less than is expected. Conversely, contributing too much could be a *faux pas,* too. In that case, one might be embarrassing one's neighbors.

This method of collecting money for local purposes is not limited to the school. The local shrines are supported in the same way, as are specific local projects. During the author's stay, one large *buraku* was raising money through voluntary assessments to pay for the paving of its main street. Each family living along the street was assessed more than the families living away from it, but all households in the *buraku* were supposed to contribute. Much discussion occurred about the amounts that would be expected from each household. The political leadership and shopkeepers were expected to be especially generous.

On the other hand, when collections are taken up for such organizations as the Tokai Town shrine, the Nichū school, as an organization, is expected to contribute, as well as the principal and head teacher. While the author watched, a representative paid a visit to the principal to collect his donation for the Tokai Town shrine. After looking at the list of contributions already collected, the principal conferred with the head teacher and the school clerk about the amount the school would contribute. The administrators also had to give a personal donation. The head teacher was probably tapped again because he is also a resident of the shrine district.

Thus the Nichū PTA carries out its *kōenkai* (school supporters' organization) functions in the traditional way of local community organizations and relies upon community solidarity to enforce sanctions that make the legally voluntary system socially obligatory.

As a formal organization, the Nichū PTA had no regular membership list. By definition, all parents of Nichū pupils are automatically members of the PTA and their membership dues are a part of the monthly fees collected from each child.

A general PTA meeting is scheduled toward the beginning of the school year when officers are elected and budgets approved in formal session. About one hundred and eighty parents came to the meeting in April 1962, representing roughly one fourth of the pupils' families. At the general meeting, mothers predominated, though men delegated as *buraku-ku* representatives (*riji*) to the Nichū

PTA Council also came. The meeting began with extensive greetings from the principal and the PTA chairman. The chairman was specifically concerned with the national achievement tests first given in the preceding year in which the prefectural average had been close to the bottom for the nation. He expressed his desire for much effort on the part of school, parents, and pupils to do better in the coming year. The principal reminded parents that the third-year pupils faced intensified competition for high school entrance because of the postwar "baby boom" peak. Giving his recommendations for home study, he said first-year pupils should study independently one or more hours a day, second-year pupils two or more hours a day, while third-year pupils would necessarily have to study for longer hours in order to keep up with their classes *and* review for their high school entrance examinations.

The business session began with the chairman calling for a review of the PTA budget. All parents had brought previously distributed mimeographed copies of the PTA budget to the meeting. They appeared to look them over carefully. The school clerk, who serves as the PTA treasurer, made a long explanation of the budget items and two auditors (regular PTA officers) confirmed their inspection of the report.

Though the chairman gave ample time and encouragement for questionning of the treasurer's report, there was only one short question and desultory side conversation. The chairman called for separate approval of the treasurer's final report of the preceding year and the proposed budget for the coming year. A few voices of assent could be heard, so the reports were declared approved.

Then the meeting was turned over to a younger PTA official who had been given the job of chairing the election of officers for the coming year. Appointed by the principal, he, in turn, appointed a nominating committee which included several older men and the head teacher. They left the meeting, but returned after a ten-minute conference to propose a single slate of officers. On their return, the oldest man, in typical Japanese fashion, was appointed to read the results of the meeting. He read the names of the officers selected. This constituted the election; no vote was taken. However, the old man had difficulty reading his list and had to be prompted by the principal, who had *not* been in the nominating meeting, but was obviously aware of who the intended officers were to be. With the principal's prompting, the entire list of officials was finally read.

Without comment or disturbance, the nominations were accepted. All officers, except one, were re-elected to positions which they had held the previous year. One Uena farmer was substituted by the nominating committee for another farmer as a vice-chairman.

The chairman responded with obvious enthusiasm to his reelection and said he "would be happy to serve again." His reelection was occasion for another speech and repeated mention of his hopes for better prefectural achievement on the coming national tests.

The officers elected were (1) the chairman, owner of six factories (Tokai); (2) five vice-chairmen: a retired insurance man (Tokai), daughter-in-law of the Nippon City mayor (Tokai), a doctor (Uena), an ex-landlord farmer (Uena), and the

Nichū Principal; (3) two auditors: a hardware dealer (Tokai) and an ex-landlord farmer (Uena); (4) treasurer: the Nichū school clerk; and (5) secretary: the Nichū head teacher.

The chairman and one of the vice-chairmen had no children in Nichū during the 1962–1963 school year. This election was the fourteenth successive time that the Chairman had been elected to his position.

It is not unusual in Japan for PTA officers to be chosen who have no children in the school concerned. In many cases, the expectation is that such a position will lead to local political office. The Nichū PTA chairman has not shown any inclination to run for political office, but obviously enjoyed the honors accorded his local position.

The PTA general meeting was scheduled to close with a speech by a social education consultant from the prefectural education office. He arrived while the business session was still proceeding and waited his turn to speak. Once given the floor he spoke for more than an hour about the problems that parents face in raising teenagers in contemporary Japanese society. The parents listened attentively and then were dismissed.

The parents' participation in the meeting had been passive. A slate of candidates, obviously selected prior to the formation of the nominating committee by the top school and PTA officials, was granted formal approval in an outwardly democratic manner, not uncommon in local Japanese organizations (Cf. Dore 1958:414–26).

THE PTA COUNCIL

Besides the ten officers elected at the general meeting, the PTA has one to six representatives (*riji*) selected by each *buraku-ku,* hamlet or neighborhood, who meet together several times a year as a PTA Council (*rijikai*). Though most schools have far smaller PTA councils, Nichū has 66 *buraku-ku* representatives. All but one are parents of Nichū students. The effective "steering committee" is the group of ten elected officers, who meet frequently at the school. Even among the elected officers, there is some feeling that the organization is dominated by the PTA chairman and the principal who settle problems and set policy, only asking other officers and the PTA Council to ratify their decisions.

The Council's functions, as described by the Nichū head teacher, are (1) to consult with the school on large projects, particularly those that will require community donations to carry them out, (2) to attend two general meetings a year, (3) to collect donations at the time of special drives from all of the households in their community, and (4) to prepare the PTA budget for approval at the next general meeting.

Special PTA committees, responsible to the council, are appointed from among the representatives (*riji*) or other community leaders. The committees are (1) the welfare committee (*koseiiinkai*) whose major responsibility is the organization of food and refreshment sales at the annual school athletic meeting (a money-raising project) (2) the guidance committee (*hodoiinkai*) which has the responsibility of organizing local recreational programs during the school vacations and communicating school concerns to the local community about pupil behavior during these periods, (3) the adult committee (*seijiniinkai*) which is consulted in the arrangements for special programs for parents at the school (adult classes or lectures), (4) the association for the support of high school entrance (*shingaku kōenkai*) which arranges for the financial support of extracurricular review classes (*kagai*) at the school for children who plan to take the high school entrance examinations, and (5) the sports supporters' association (*taiiku kōenkai*) which arranges for financial support of Nichū athletic teams and helps obtain volunteer coaches for some of the sports. The latter two *kōenkai* organizations have budgets separate from the PTA, but function more in the fashion of the other committees than as separate organizations.

During the 1962–1963 school year, the PTA Council met three times. The first meeting occurred three weeks after the general PTA meeting for all parents, at which officers had been elected. About forty members appeared at the school meeting which was similar in style to the larger one that preceded it. The women sat at the back of the meeting room, while the men sat on the sides. The officers sat at the front facing the rest of the membership.

Short speeches by the chairman and the principal opened the meeting. The principal commented that two problems faced by the middle school were (1) the heavy concentration of children in the third-year class across the nation leading to intense competition for available high school openings and (2) the national increase in crimes by middle school age children. Relating this to the local situation, he said, "Some children have already gone to the movies ten or twenty times in the first month of school, hardly even coming to school or doing their work."

Then, the chairman gave out special certificates and gifts (*kinenhin*) to three community residents who were being honored for their past services to the PTA. Only the recently replaced vice-chairman, an old Uena farmer, was there to receive his gift and make a short speech of appreciation. Introduction of all the officers and representatives followed with the chairman setting the pattern, "I'm Tanabe." After introduction of the American researcher who would be studying the community and school for the coming year, the meeting was declared closed by the head teacher.

Immediately following that statement, however, he formally declared the opening of the sports supporters' association (*taiiku kōenkai*) and the chairman of that group came forward to chair the meeting. The association chairman was the vice-chairman of the Nippon City Council and a local shopkeeper of Uena Region. He gave a short speech and then called for the reading of the budget reports by the treasurer.

A Nichū physical education teacher read and explained the mimeographed budget that had been distributed, dealing with the purchase of athletic supplies and provision of funds for intramural and inter-scholastic sports competitions. No questions were asked. Grunts of approval from two or three council members sitting near the front indicated the budgets were approved. One old woman, more vocal than the rest, said, "I think that's fine."

The meeting was turned over to the head teacher who proceeded to describe the timetable for the construction of the new Nichū gymnasium, a subject that brought much applause. The head teacher suggested, after the sports supporters' association chairman had left the room, that he be retained as chairman, a suggestion that was accepted without dissent. The head teacher was then able to formally announce the close of the meeting.

The PTA Council meeting thus consisted of passive participation by representatives who listened to both school authorities and PTA officers run through their scheduled program. Separation of the two meetings had been a legalistic fiction to preserve a separate legal identity for the PTA and the sports supporters' association.

Immediately following the meeting, the head teacher invited all present to adjourn to another school classroom where a party had been laid out. With the purpose of "getting acquainted," a traditional *sake*-drinking party had been planned by the principal. *Sake* and *sashimi* (raw sliced fish) had been put out in individual servings on tables improvised from student desks. No hesitation was expressed, and teachers and council members immediately moved into the party room. Described as "country hospitality," the party would not have been held in city schools, according to one teacher.

After everyone had found a seat and was awaiting the formal opening of the party, the PTA chairman stood up to announce a toast. Everyone reached out for the small bottles of warmed *sake* and proceeded to pour as many of his neighbors' cups as he could reach. To fill one's own cup was not considered proper. Then, when everyone had been served, there was a general expression of *kampai,* led by the chairman as an opening toast. Prior to the toast, everyone had been sitting quietly, waiting for the officials at the head table to make the first move. But the beginning of drinking also signalled the immediate drop of conventional social embarrassment with strangers and acquaintances and the beginning of animated conversation around a number of topics. Teachers sat together in small groups among the parents but talked more with each other than with the parents.

After the first two cups of *sake,* men began to express friendship by handing their own *sake* cup to a neighbor, filling the cup for him, and encouraging him to drink. Often, the cup would be drained and returned to the giver, symbolizing an exchange of friendship. The principal made a point of moving around the room and exchanging cups with a number of the officers and parents present. The women, sitting at the back of the room, were given a bottle of wine and some soft drinks, since they were not expected to enjoy drinking *sake.*

As the party proceeded, there were many friendly interchanges and little sign of inhibition or embarrassment, even on the part of the women. There was a noticeable progression from the stiffness of the formal meeting preceding the first toast to the end of the party when the head teacher began to sing traditional folk songs. The women excused themselves about halfway through the party, but most of the men stayed on to enjoy the occasion. Much joking and laughter was evident. There was no formal ending to the party, rather, a gradual drifting out of the guests. As a stylized pattern of the local society, such a party was always described as an occa-

Nichū PTA councilmen at party dedicating the new Nichū gymnasium.

sion for the "development of good relations among people." Such parties occurred frequently throughout the school year with different sets of participants.

Occasions for such parties involving representatives of the local community were (1) after the entrance ceremony for new pupils when the teachers and PTA officers met to plan coming activities and to bid farewell to two teachers who were being transferred to other schools with the opening of the new school year; (2) after the first PTA Council meeting described above; (3) after the annual school athletic meet, for the teachers and all the parents who had participated in the arrangements; (4) at the ceremony celebrating the raising of the roofbeams of the new gymnasium when a Shinto priest performed the appropriate rites and PTA officers sat down with the teachers and construction workers inside the new framework to participate in the traditional party for the workers; (5) at the dedication of the new gymnasium when all the PTA Council members and people of importance in the community were invited to attend; (6) at the New Year's period when a traditional beginning-of-the-new-year party was combined with a farewell celebration for the departing American researcher, to which many of the PTA Council members and teachers were invited; and (7) the party following the graduation ceremony in March when the PTA Council members paid their respects to the teachers' efforts during the past year.

In addition, almost any party involving the Nichū School was not considered complete without the participation of the chairman and one or more of the PTA vice-chairmen, regardless of the connection with PTA activities. Parties, however, did not follow parents' meetings (*fukeikai*) which were called for the purpose of group and individual guidance or instruction.

THE GUIDANCE COMMITTEE

The Nichū PTA guidance committee (*hodoiinkai*) held meetings preceding the summer and winter vacation periods. Each *buraku-ku* group sent one or more parents to represent their neighborhood at these meetings. Some *riji* (PTA Council representatives) also served as guidance committee representatives. Similar in form to other PTA activities already described, the general purpose of the committee meetings was to convey to the local *buraku* and *ku* groups the school's concerns for pupil behavior during the vacation periods. Indicating the importance attached to these meetings, the PTA chairman attended, though he had no official responsibility on the committee.

Arriving late for the first meeting, he had to wait to give his speech until the principal had finished. The head teacher, as master of ceremonies, introduced the chairman's speech with an apology that it was only because the chairman was late that his place on the program followed the principal's. This was a clear indication of the chairman's higher social rank even within the school setting. When both were present, the chairman generally spoke first.

The chairman of the guidance committee, in his turn, got up only to apologize for the inconvenience caused the delegates in the holding of the meeting. A bicycle shopkeeper from Uena Region, he was newly-chosen for the committee chairmanship. The meeting had been programmed and arranged by the Nichū principal and head teacher.

Specific concerns were expressed by the principal in the planning of activities for children during the six-week vacation. In general, he was concerned about what the children would be up to when they were away from home and school. Specifically, he warned about the children (1) riding motorcycles, prohibited by law until they were older, (2) swimming in dangerous, unguarded places, (3) walking around the urban center of Nippon City, without specific business, where they could be lured into all kinds of mischief from playing pinball machines (*pachinko*) to petty thievery, (4) going to the movie theaters and getting into trouble there or seeing "bad" movies, (5) getting into trouble after the summer festivals when the older youth do a lot of drinking and try to tempt the younger middle school students into drinking and smoking, and (6) walking alone at night, for the girls, when they might be taken off for a motorcycle ride by the older boys. "Of course, only a small part of our 826 pupils will get into trouble like this," he concluded.

The chairman emphasized that parents should be strict with their children and be sure to follow the wishes of the school with respect to their children's activities for the summer.

Pupil *buraku-ku* group officers were also present at the meeting. At the end of the meeting, they were asked to plan, with the parent-representatives and teachers assigned to their *buraku-ku* group, summer recreational activities in their respective neighborhoods. The *buraku-ku* groups were asked to form separate "buzz sessions" to make these plans.

When the general committee meeting reconvened about one-half hour later, the parents were asked if they had any questions or suggestions. One woman asked about the use of the new Nippon City swimming pool which was being reserved during the summer for the different city schools on a group basis. This brought some discussion of a summer swimming schedule that had been prepared by the school. Otherwise, there were no suggestions directed at the school.

During the meeting, the school, backed by the PTA officials, had told the parents, through the parent *buraku-ku* representatives, about the kinds of recreational activities that should be planned on a local neighborhood basis. In addition, they were being given a series of admonitions about what should and should not be allowed in the way of individual summer activity for children. A list of specific regulations was passed out that reflected, in detail, the principal's talk. "Students should not go to the urban center of Nippon City unless accompanied by an adult," was the kind of regulation being laid down in the name of the school and the PTA. Responsibility for the guidance of pupils' out-of-school recreational activities was accepted by all as the normal responsibility of the school. Similar lists of rules for children's behavior were prepared by one of the teachers and handed out to *buraku-ku* representatives at the winter meeting of the guidance committee.

The major theme of the rules is the pupil's home life and his responsibilities to his family. Of the four sections of rules for pupils, only one is concerned with academic home study relavent to the school's academic program. The rest of the sections —"living in a proper, well-regulated way," "keeping in good health," and "enjoying a bright family life"—are concerned with responsibilities to home and family. By extension, these areas of conduct are made a responsibility of the pupil to the school in the Nichū District. Of interest in light of the parents' frequently expressed desire for stricter (*kibishii*) teachers, the school includes a request to the parents to be stricter in the discipline of their children.

"Directions for the Family," the list of rules passed out for winter vacation guidance of children, follows the same types of emphases as the rules issued to the children directly. It is not difficult to understand the plaintive statement of one mother who said during the home interview, "When I was a child, we were told by our teachers to think of our parents above everything else; now the teachers tell us as parents to think of our children above everything else." Perhaps teachers have always emphasized the need for obedience to parents when talking with children and the need for careful upbringing and discipline of children when talking with parents.

The school authorities seem to be especially concerned about the possibility of the children falling into the company of delinquents. The children are told, in the rules mentioned above, not to go to movies unless "approved" by the school or unless they go with their family. "Approved" movies are seen on these occasions, at least once in a school term, when all of the pupils are taken to the movie theatre by the teachers as an outing from school. There were no other "school-approved" movies.

THE YOUTH PROBLEMS COUNCIL

Further evidence of the concern for guidance of children outside the school occurred in the formation of a new organization, independent of the guidance committee, during the period of this study. About a week after the guidance committee's winter meeting, many officials gathered at Nichū to inaugurate the Nippon City Nichū District Youth Health, Protection, and Rearing Drive Committee (*Seishōnen Kenzen Hogo Ikusei Iinkai*) or the Youth Problems Council (*Seishōnen Mondai Kyogikai*) as it was called by the participants. Prior to the meeting, invitations had been issued by the Nichū principal to all teachers and PTA officers of Nichū District, members of the PTA guidance and adult education committees of the three schools, to Mothers Association and Womens Association leaders, to members of the Nippon City Youth Problems Council, and to every *buraku-ku* headman in the district. (The chairman of the Nichū PTA guidance committee did not appear, nor had he been included in the planning.) In attendance, also, were the Nippon City superintendent of education, one of the city Board of Education supervisors, a local member of the Board of Education, representatives from the city police station and the city public welfare office, and the principals of the three Nichū District schools. The meeting was generally well-attended.

Two years before, formation of a similar organization at one of the other Nippon City middle schools had been credited with reducing the incidence of juvenile delinquency in its area. Local officials of the Board of Education, Welfare Office, and Police Station were anxious to organize the entire city in the same manner. Though Nichū District had few problems with delinquency, the organization had to be formed. The meeting opened with a short talk by the Nichū principal in which he played up the speech to be given by the police representative and the problem of smoking among middle school students. "Only two children used to smoke before, but now they have passed the habit on to their friends and ten children are smokers." He explained that the different middle school districts of the city were all starting similar organizations to promote cooperation between the schools, the Welfare Office, and the Board of Education. "Now we want to start this here and we want to ask for your cooperation and understanding. We have the aim of making a bright (*akarui*) Tokai, a bright Uena, and bright schools."

The principal was followed by the welfare office representative and the Nippon City superintendent of education. Both men painted a glowing picture of how an organization such as they proposed could help youth and prevent crime. The superintendent drew organization charts on the blackboard to show that the Nichū District Youth Problems Council would be a sub-group of the Nippon City Youth Problems Council, headed by the mayor, and part of regional and national organizations with the same name. He cited the organization formed at another Nippon City middle school, mentioned above, as a model of what could be accomplished. The PTA guidance committee was described as carrying the central responsibility for meeting community responsibility to youth.

When the speeches were concluded, a business meeting ensued. A slight change in the formal name of the organization was made and officers were elected. Chairman of the new organization was to be the Nichū PTA chairman and the two assistant chairmen were to be the respective PTA chairmen of the two elementary schools. The meeting ended with the Nichū principal passing out copies of "Winter Vacation Family Guidance."

The author was not able to observe any further activities of the new council. Presumably, it was developed more as a formality than as an operating organization in the manner of the separate sports supporters' association that meets as a part of the Nichū PTA Council. The guidance committee will possibly receive more prestige in the community and will be emphasized more by the school officials. By making the three PTA chairmen from the Nichū District schools officers of the new organization the council becomes an adjunct of the already existing PTA organization.

ASSOCIATION FOR THE SUPPORT OF HIGH SCHOOL ENTRANCE

As a separate organization, not officially under the PTA, the association for the support of high school entrance has been formed to encourage school efforts to get as many children as possible into the prestige high schools. All third-year pupil parents who want their children to continue their education after middle school graduation are automatic members. Like the PTA, the major activity is fund raising. A special assessment of 250 yen per month per high school aspirant is collected by the *buraku-ku* representatives of the association. Most of the money is used to pay a special bonus to the teachers responsible for third-year pupil guidance and the extracurricular review classes that they teach for the high school aspirants. A part of the preparation for high school entrance examinations consists of monthly tests put out by a private prefectural organization. All high school aspirants take these tests and the scores are used to determine to which high school an individual should apply. The tests are designed in the same form as the actual high school entrance tests and are scored by a central office which tabulates scores for the entire prefecture, allowing teachers to know the ranks of their pupils on a prefecture-wide basis. The practice testing service is expensive and the costs are taken out of funds of the association for the support of high school entrance.

The officers of the association are generally PTA officers who are elected to a position when their own children are in the third-year class. The president, during the period of this study, was one of the three PTA vice-chairmen, the retired insurance man from Tokai Town. The treasurer was a Tokai shopkeeper who served as a PTA councilman.

Meetings of the association are the occasion for Nichū teachers to talk with parents about the problems of high school entrance and to keep the parents informed on their children's progress. At the first meeting in May, the teacher responsible for coordinating high school entrance guidance spent an hour and a half explaining to the parents the problems involved and the plans for the year. Much attention was given to the numbers of children who had been able to gain admittance to each of the local high schools in preceding years and the relative difficulties in gaining admittance. This discussion included the number of points that would be required on the final entrance examination for each school, based on the standings of the previous years. Though none of this information is supposed to be made public by the high schools or middle schools, it is, indeed, public knowledge. The teacher stressed, also, that two to three hours of review study every day was necessary to prepare for the tests.

About 180 parents attended the meeting. After the first talk, they broke up into *buraku-ku* groups to make arangements for the collection of dues and for local activities. Then they came together again for a desultory business meeting with the inevitable approval of the budget and ratification of officers selected for the association. Proper nominating form and democratic procedure, however, were used.

At the end of the official meeting, parents met their children's teachers by classroom groups. The small meetings included additional explanation of the testing procedures followed by individual consultations with each parent.

Though this was only one of many occasions for parent-teacher consultations during the crucial third-year planning for the children's future after middle school graduation, the parents waited patiently for their turns to talk with the teachers. The last interviews were after 6 P.M., a long wait for parents who had come to the meeting five hours previously.

A second general meeting of the association was called in late January when the results of the practice, "imitation (*mogi*) test," given earlier that month, had been returned to the schools. The results of this test represented the final scores available before submission of high school applications, and were, thus, most important in the final determination of an appropriate school for a borderline pupil. At the time of the meeting, parents were informed of their children's scores and given final guidance before the high school applications were to be made out. A significant feature of the meeting was the presence of representatives from each of the local high schools to which Nichū graduates generally go in large numbers. Either the principals or head teachers come to talk about the types of courses their high schools offer, the degree of difficulty in entrance, costs, etc.

After the association had paid the teachers their appropriate end-of-year bonuses, the rest of the budget was used to finance an appreciation *sake* party for the teachers to be given immediately after the graduation ceremony.

The teachers involved with the third-year students exert much effort to ensure that the students get into the best educational channels for which they can qualify. One of the association's purposes is to reward the teachers for their extra efforts. "If there wasn't an association, the teachers wouldn't put as much strength into their work," said the chairman of the association, emphasizing that it was a parents' organization, not one started by the school or teachers. In private interviews the president and the treasurer stressed the financial purpose of the association.

THE PTA OFFICIALS

For the most part, school officials took the initiative and made arrangements for activities included in the different PTA committees. The PTA chairman also exerted considerable influence, spending a good deal of time at the school in both ceremonial and active roles. Other PTA officers remarked on the dominant role of the chairman and the principal in decisions related to the school.

One Uena farmer, commenting on his past experiences as a PTA councilman said:

> There were so many people at a council meeting, that even though I have my own opinions, I didn't speak up. We just had a chance to say 'approve'

along with the majority. The principal would open the meeting and tell what was needed—like a new classroom or special equipment. If the principal thought it was necessary, I would agree. If the required donations were too large, I was in for a hard time. No, I never disagreed—I just didn't speak up in those meetings. I always went along with the majority.

A Tokai shopkeeper, talking about the PTA, began to describe the way that the old men (*genrō*) of Tokai Town made all the decisions, leaving little room for initiative by the younger men. The PTA chairman's power over the Nichū PTA was an example of this community pattern to him.

Because the PTA obviously wielded some degree of power in school affairs, a separate interview survey was made of fifteen elected PTA officers and the more active council members. They were asked questions similar in content to the general questions in the earlier survey of parents.

These interviews were designed to elicit general opinions about the school and its role in the community. The interview schedule did not include questions about future plans for children of the parents being interviewed as in the survey of parents described earlier. A general theme common to most of the interviews was the importance of morals education in the school and the present weakness of the public schools in this field when compared with the prewar schools. However, concerns about academic preparation for the high school entrance examinations were expressed only rarely. Such concerns had been elicited from parents in the previous survey mainly when they were talking about plans for the future of their children.

There was no agreement among the fifteen officials interviewed on the present role of morals instruction compared to the prewar morals course (*shūshin*). When asked to compare the prewar *shūshin* with the present course of *dōtoku* (morals education), eight officials though the old *shūshin* would be appropriate today, two thought that a part of it would be still appropriate, and five emphasized the separate aims of the two morals education courses in rejecting *shūshin* for children today.

Thus, emphasis upon morals education did not mean agreement on the morals appropriate for the present age or the methods of transmitting them. Conflicting social ideals were evident in the interview responses of the different officials. A well-educated official emphasized the necessity of teaching good ideals of sportsmanship, spirit, and individual responsibility. He took opposition to the idea that patriotism and love of country (*aikokushin*) should be taught in moral education. But five officials considered patriotism an important part of moral education. One suggested that the kind of national loyalty taught by the Boy Scouts is very important. Six officials thought that children should be taught to respect their superiors, but none mentioned preservation of the Japanese family system as a goal.

The PTA chairman was by far the most outspoken, critical, and politically conservative person interviewed. Accustomed to his role of aggressive social and business leadership, he was not reluctant about voicing criticism of the United States' role in shaping postwar Japanese educational organization and practice. The extension of compulsory education from six to nine years and the change from the prewar multi-track system of schools beyond the elementary grades were subjects of great concern to him. The less able students, which he estimated as one third of those presently in Nichū, were forced, he felt, to continue an academic education for which they were unsuited. Such "trash" (*kuzu*) should not interfere with the education of the more able students and should be put to productive work. He called the system "a great loss to the Japanese economy" and a "useless respect for human rights." In his view, the middle school should have continued as the exclusive channel to higher education that it had been before the war.

Looking back to the prewar system of Japanese education, he felt that the present system could be reformed only as it was remolded into the image of the past. In this, he compared the Japanese reaction to the occupation with that of Germany. The Germans, he said, had resisted the educational changes urged on them by Americans. "West Germany is a far better model for Japan than the United States."

To him, prewar *shūshin* represented the ideal educational goal. There was no part of it which he would now reject. "*Shūshin* was an ideal for a human being from birth to death . . . it was a perfect ideal for an excellent and honorable *rippa na*) person . . . All people who have received *shūshin* education are spiritually rich . . . I would certainly like to bring it back by all means."

In describing the prewar school system, he emphasized the unity which it had brought to the Japanese people.

"If anybody was told to die, happily he went to the battlefield and died for the glory of his homeland. . . . A hundred million hearts beating as one (*ichioku isshin*). These (examples) are from the prewar period. This is the very expression of education. This is what I positively believe."

Throughout the interview, he gave no indication of being sensitive to the criticism of prewar schools or the fears of an educational "reverse course" held by the Japan Teachers Union. In no sense did he repudiate the militaristic background of Japan's educational development, or the role of the schools in preparation for war. He clearly stated his own personal identification with the conservative course of the Ministry of Education.

There was a strong element of puritanical ideal evident in both this interview and the actions of the PTA chairman. His youngest son, a student at the Ichikō high school, was allowed to use only a canvas bag while his classmates from poorer homes carried leather briefcases. The chairman's home was unpretentious and his wife employed no household help. Conspicuous donation to local causes, rather than conspicuous consumption, was the chairman's practice. He had recently contributed a large inscribed monument to the war dead of Tokai Town. It stood in front of the Tokai shrine. The Chinese characters of the donor's name were twice as large as the characters used in recording the names of the World War II casualties, and had been placed in the most prominent position. Large donations were given to both Nichū and the Tokai Elementary School. Newspapers recorded contributions to a local Red Cross hospital. Benevolences of various kinds were granted to a variety of local organizations. The rumor circulated that he made the heaviest political contributions to the mayor's election campaign fund.

During the interview, the chairman described a recent situation in which he had slapped his son hard on the cheek. The punishment was given because the boy had left home for school without first folding up his bedding and putting it in the closet. The description of punishing his child was the only one heard by the author directly from a parent. Nichū parents generally did not expect to discipline their own children in this way, though some expected the school to do so. Such practice, in fact, was usually associated with prewar teachers. The chairman not only described administering such punishment himself, but was indignant about postwar teachers who refused to do the same thing at school.

> The principal now is shallow and frivilous; he has too much regard for the pupil's feelings. If I speak bluntly to the teachers, they always reply, 'There is a Fundamental Law of Education. According to it, we cannot do so. We understand what you are saying, chairman, but we cannot do it because of the Fundamental Law of Education.' For instance, I tell the teachers that we must apply discipline in order to carefully educate the citizens of the future, but teachers say they cannot do this because of the Fundamental Law of Education.[1]

In such statements the chairman was expressing disgust both for the American-introduced innovations in the school system and for the postwar teachers who did not fulfill his expectations of their community responsibility.

In this, his orientation to the local community was made very explicit. At one point he expressed his opinion that teachers should not be transferred frequently between different communities and schools, but should stay in one community until they become a part of its soil (*tsuchi ni naru*); that is, until they die. "Rolling around and shifting (schools) too often is no good."

In a different context he referred to the Nippon City students who went to public or private high schools in Tokyo.

"Of those students who commute to school in Tokyo, out of one hundred, all are 'zeroes'. If they go to Tokyo and don't attend local schools, their grades are bad, even those in the university. They are forced to do this—forced to it by their parents' vanity."

To his way of thinking, only those schools in the local community that were staffed by teachers who had a long period of residence in the community, could provide the conservative moral and academic education he desired. No conflict was recognized in the moral and academic goals, though he expressed the desire for an exclusive middle school with entrance examinations.

When asked about the teachers' union, the chairman responded vehemently that he was "completely opposed."

"Teachers should be what they are. . . . The teacher must regard his job as a holy calling, a noble occupation, and society should regard it in the same way. That is the way it was before. Now if a person cannot get some other kind of job, he becomes a teacher for a while. Even trash can become teachers."

Later, he went on to say that because Japan was again independent, the system should be changed. "The Japan Teachers Union does not fit the conditions of Japan."

It was obvious that the chairman's personal views were not representative of all

---

[1] The Fundamental Law of Education includes nothing about corporal punishment.

the PTA officials. Though he felt very strongly that the middle school should not be a part of the compulsory education period in Japan, only two other officials of the fifteen interviewed expressed a similar feeling. Eight officials felt that the present system of compulsory education through the middle school was good. Four more officials felt that high schools should become a part of the system, at least to the extent that all children who desired a high school education would be accommodated in the public high schools.

On the other hand, the chairman's opinions about the Japan Teachers Union was shared by seven other officials to the extent that they did not believe in a teachers' union. Only one official ventured the opinion that it was good to have a teachers' union and that it did not matter if the teachers sometimes disobeyed the directives of the Ministry of Education.

"I don't admire the Japan Teachers Union's political activities, but the situation is better than before. It is good that there is a union. If the teachers are opposed to the policies of the Ministry of Education, they don't always have to be obedient."

In speaking specifically of Japan Teachers Union and Ministry of Education disputes at the national level, five officials expressed agreement with the objectives of the Ministry, while four took the position that both parties were to blame. No one supported only the Japan Teachers Union position. The officials either specified a personal preference for the conservative Liberal Democratic Party or else avoided replying to a direct question of political party preference.

Besides the chairman, eight of the PTA officials expressed a concern for the lack of stricter teachers. "Liberalism has been bad for the children," said one man. Another complained, "The teachers used to feel pride about 'making men' (*hito o tsukuru*); it was more important than academic studies. Now that they love the children too much, they don't really produce strong people."

When asked for comments as to which part of the curriculum needed strengthening, seven of the fifteen officers declined to answer. On this aspect of the school, they did not feel qualified to comment. "I'm not an educationist and so can't answer," said one. Another seven officers cited the English language as a subject that should be given greater emphasis, but only two mentioned the teaching of Japanese language. The chairman compared schools he had visited recently in China with the local schools, and commented that the teaching of Chinese language and writing was far more advanced in China than the teaching of Chinese language and characters to Japanese students.

One of the officials included in the survey lacked a formal position in the Nichū PTA, but was a member of the Nippon City Board of Education and lived in the Nichū district. He was the formal representative of the Board at all Nichū functions that required such representation. As a neighbor of the mayor and an old, respected farmer, he carried some weight in the PTA activities. While expressing a moderately conservative view with respect to the school and its role in the community, he was the only person surveyed who perceived an inherent conflict between the aims of morals education and the school's emphasis on preparation for academic entrance examinations.

The present examination system is very bad. We had exams before but not to the extent of today. The tests for high school and university entrance are all-important and there is no time left in school for morals education . . . All members of the Board of Education think that the present examination system is bad.

Two other officials complained about the emphasis on entrance examination preparation in the school, but did not relate this to the problem of morals education. They both suggested that the middle school was becoming a "cram school" in preparation for high school entrance and that the high school was a "cram school" in preparation for university entrance. On the other hand, the chairman of the association which supported high school entrance felt that preparation for the entrance examination was very important. His committee's job, as he described it, was to encourage the teachers to put more effort into preparing the children for their coming examinations.

PARENT-TEACHER CONFERENCES

The greatest amount of contact between teachers and the community occurred in the conferences of parents with the home room teachers responsible for their children. Such conferences occurred in several settings. Most general PTA meetings for parents at the school ended with the parents spending about five minutes each conferring with their children's home room teachers. The public setting and the pressure of time did not give much scope to such teacher-parent interaction.

Parents who did not come to the regular PTA meetings were often asked to come to school the following week for conferences. Many parents arranged, on a sporadic basis, to consult informally with a teacher after school. In some cases the teachers initiated the meeting to gain the help of parents in matters where the parents might help. More often, parents came to teachers with their concerns about preparing their children for the high school entrance examinations. Several teachers reported receiving telephone calls and visits at their homes from worried parents wishing advice.

Especially for the third-year pupils who were in the final lap of the race to high school entrance, teacher-parent conferences occurred frequently. Both parents and teachers were emotionally involved in the children's success or failure in applying for high school entrance. The problems were immediate and acute.

Two weeks after the opening of the school year and the entrance ceremony for first-year pupils, one week was set aside by the principal and teachers for visits by the teachers to the children's homes. These visits were viewed by the school staff and the parents as an occasion for private consultation about the children, a time for parent and student guidance. To make time for the visits, all pupils were dismissed from school after lunch, giving the teachers six afternoons to visit the homes of each of the fifty or so home room pupils for whom they were responsible. Each afternoon the teachers left the school, using their own bicycles and motorcycles to visit the various homes.

While it was physically impossible in the time allowed for all teachers to contact each of the fifty families of pupils for whom they were responsible, the community was covered quite thoroughly. Among the random sample of fifty-four families of third-year pupils interviewed by the author, several had never visited the school, but, with one exception, all had been in direct contact with a Nichū teacher previously. The one exceptional case was the home of a girl of low academic capability whose mother worked during the day. The author and his assistant visited the mother at home one evening, but found it difficult to get her responses to the interview questions because of her apparent lack of intelligence. The girl, however, in her home setting, exhibited none of the dull characteristics attributed to her by the teachers from their school observations.

The author accompanied several of the third-year home room teachers on their calls and was able to observe the manner of communication between teachers and parents and learn the nature of their topics of conversation. The overriding importance of the problems of high school entrance provided a counter-influence to the stultifying effect of a foreign observer on the teacher-parent interaction, though the author's only confirmation of this observation came from the post-interview comments of the teachers involved.

In most of the homes visited, children and their parents were planning on high school entrance in the following year. Topics of conversation were almost entirely related to this concern. Because of the recent start of the school year, teachers were dependent, generally, on the results of past achievement tests for evaluation of the pupils' potential chances for entrance to a particular high school. In some cases, the teachers recorded these scores and reviewed them before visiting the parents. Others simply asked the parents for their child's score and then made the evaluation.

Illustrating the social value placed upon school achievement, parent-teacher interaction patterns varied with the degree of academic success of the child. Parents whose children were in danger of not being admitted to the high school of their choice because of low grades were very nervous in their interviews and sought ways of ingratiating themselves with the teachers. The teachers were viewed as people of considerable influence in the children's future, possibly holding the powers of high school admission or nonadmission.

The teachers, in turn, conducted themselves with an air of strictness and authority in this setting, rebuffing or deprecating attempts at ingratiation by the parents. On leaving one home where the mother was very concerned about her eldest son's high school entrance, the mother attempted to give the teacher a wrapped package containing a gift. Though the author was not close at hand, it was possible to observe the teacher's rough refusal of the package, the mother's frankly desperate efforts to persuade the teacher to accept it, the teacher's final physical rejection of the gift, and the mother's distraught expression as she held it out to him. Acceptance of this package would have implied a degree of obligation on the part of the teacher which he did not wish to accept.

A general pattern of teacher counselling, observed in most of the visits, was evident in the teachers's inquiry about the home study habits of the child. The question was always asked in terms of the number of hours the pupil devoted to home study. No matter how the parent responded (and answers ranged from no home study to three hours daily of home study) the teacher would reply, "He's got to make a little more effort (*mo sukoshi gambare*). He should spend more time in home study."

In many of the homes, the parents commented that their child wanted to watch television instead of studying. They pointed out that there was conflict between parents and children over television viewing. One family indicated that they had refrained from buying a television set until after their child had passed his high school entrance examination. Others evidenced no apology for the presence of the television set in their homes but were concerned about the children's renunciation of study in favor of watching television.

A different parent-teacher conference atmosphere prevailed in the homes of children whose school records were good. In most such homes, parents and teachers were relaxed and conversed unhurriedly about a variety of subjects. The teacher fulfilled parental expectations of his role by advising a little more effort in home study. This was friendly advice, however, when compared to the severity of the same advice given in other settings.

In several homes, the child's school achievement or the family's economic situation prohibited even the thought of high school entrance. Again, the teachers were less severe, but tended to pass on the same advice about more intensive home study. In some cases this was justified by the teacher's reference to the examinations which the better companies used in selecting their employees from the middle school graduating class.

In one home visited, the son, who was a third year Nichū pupil, had been absent from school for several days. It appeared that the boy might not receive a middle school diploma if he did not attend school more often. The teacher directed the widowed mother to call the boy in. He then lectured him severely about his absence from school. When he asked the boy why he had not been in school the past two days, the boy replied that he had suffered a toothache. He showed the teacher a badly decayed tooth. The teacher became sympathetic and said, "Oh, it must have hurt very much." The boy embarassedly replied, "Oh, no." The teacher then turned on him sharply and said, "Then why didn't you come to school today?"

Later during the visit, the teacher attempted to convince the boy that he should come back to school. He inquired about employment plans for the coming year and said, "Who'll want to hire Jiro Morioka when he hasn't gone to school?"

After the visit, the author asked the teacher whether he thought the boy's behavior and school attendance would improve. The teacher's response was negative. "But at least he will think a little," he said.

In all teacher-parent conferences that the author observed, in home visits and at school, no parent appeared to be defensive or protective of his child in discussing his academic weaknesses. Instead, a parent would give encouragement to the teacher to be severe in his relations with the child. In addition, parents often asked the teachers to give their children more work, and to make them study longer hours. Similarly, the teachers were asking the parents to help them enforce better study habits and longer hours of study.

In one case, the teacher made a home visit during which he was frank with the pupil's mother about her son's academic inadequacies. The teacher ended the meeting by asking, "Should I be more severe (*kibishii*) with him?" He made a slapping gesture as if hitting the boy. The mother indicated her encouragement of physical punishment and seemed genuinely hopeful that he would use it.

Home visits had other purposes for the teachers besides counselling on academic achievement for high school entrance. Specifically, parents helped to familiarize the teachers with the home environment of their students. In one of the families visited, the pupil had not yet bought his required textbooks. In the course of conversation with his mother, the teacher indicated that he would make arrangements to have her PTA monthly fees waived, so that she could spend the money saved to buy the boy's textbooks. She appeared obviously relieved by this arrangement.

High school entrance and attendance requires a certain minimum of school expenses which must be borne by the family. National scholarships are awarded to a very few, needy children of exceptional academic ability on the basis of a special scholarship examination. The students from the poorest homes, however, have little chance of completing high schoool, even when they are able to pass their entrance examinations. For these families, it is usually imperative that children who have graduated from the middle school find work and contribute to their family's income. In one case, an academically poor student who should have been a third-year pupil lived by himself and worked full-time for his own support. The school made no effort to enforce his attendance.

NEW YEAR'S DAY

Direct observation of the school's position in the Nippon City social structure was possible on New Year's Day, the time for traditional visits to one's superiors in Japanese society. It is a time when family members gather at the home of the family head and when subordinates in business and politics pay respects to their chief.

Though the New Year's celebration extends over several days, the formal and important visits were made on January 1. In the morning, all the middle school pupils came to Nichū school, while elementary pupils went to their respective school for a short ceremony, though winter vacation had already begun. The teachers came dressed in their best suits, the head teacher with striped trousers, and the principal with striped trousers and morning coat. The pupils' uniforms were all well-washed and their buttons were polished. An assembly of pupils was held in front of the school and the principal talked to the pupils for about half an hour. His speech was a moral exhortation, during which he told the pupils that they should become as noble as the PTA chairman or the Nichū graduate who was a professional baseball star.

"You can become a scholar, an engineer, or a farmer," he told the boys and justified each as an honorable occupation. A similar list of jobs awaited the girls. But, he pointed out, one's success in life and future in all occupations would depend on his daily study and his continuing spirit of sincerity.

Immediately following the principal's exhortation, sweet cakes, made in the shape of the school's emblem, were distributed to all the children. They were then allowed to return home. Afterwards, the teachers assembled formally in the teachers' room and sat at their desks while *sake* was poured into teacups for all present.

It was a ceremonial, rather than social, occasion because only one round of *sake* was poured. This marked the only time that the author observed *sake* served at the teachers' desks. The principal drank his *sake* quickly and then left to represent the school at the annual Nippon City meeting for the exchange of name cards sponsored by the mayor. The head teacher, along with three of the older teachers, went a little bit later to the same meeting. The other teachers dispersed quickly to return home and carry out their family responsibilities.

The annual Nippon City meeting referred to above was informally called the mayor's New Year's meeting and included representatives of all government and business organizations in the city. It was a large meeting seemingly designed to enable the city's leading citizens to carry out their responsibility for a New Year's call on the mayor. The meeting relieved them, and the mayor, of the necessity of giving and receiving name cards on New Year's day since the names of all attenders were printed in a small pamphlet that was distributed to all present. All city schools, including the prefecture-administered high schools, sent their principals and a few representative teachers to the meeting. For one hour the group listened to speeches extolling the merits and future of Nippon City, and then quickly drank *sake* together. At the end, there were three cheers for Nippon City and the meeting promptly dispersed. Everyone had stood at long tables, since no seats had been provided, hence, there was little chance for extended sociability.

The Nichū principal and teacher-representatives then went to the principal's home for New Year's dinner. The head teacher explained that the entertainment by the principal was intended for the small group as representatives of the entire school staff. Over a leisurely meal, much *sake* was downed, but it was evident that the teachers were restraining their drinking in order to take care of their remaining responsibilities of the day.

After the meal, gifts designated for the mayor and the PTA chairman were brought out of a closet. The inscription on the wrappings indicated that they were from the Nichū school. The dinner guests then drove by taxi to the mayor's home in a rural hamlet within the Nichū District. Two parties were going on simultaneously in the mayor's house—one for the mayor's neighbors and one for those who were coming to call on the mayor. Gifts were presented to the mayor who made much fuss over the honored American guest who accompanied the Nichū teachers. He called for his chauffeur and car after an hour's social visit when they were ready to proceed to the next stop. Sociable interaction, rather than ceremonial exchange, was the dominant theme.

The second visit was to the PTA chairman's house. The chairman's wife was busily serving *sake* and New Year's delicacies to visitors, though the Mayor had hired the staff of the leading local restaurant for the day to serve his visitors. The Nichū teacher delegation relaxed noticeably and began to participate more freely in the festivities of the day, particularly in the consumption of the *sake* offered by the chairman.

Significantly, the chairman entertained not only the Nichū teacher delegation, but also the principals of the two elementary schools in Nichū District and the former principal of Nichū who had moved to an elementary school in a different section of the city. On New Year's Day, it was obvious that the chairman felt as closely connected to the schools of his local district as to the large business enterprise which he headed. Representatives of both groups were included in his visitors.

AN ORGANIZATION IS FORMED

One community organization related to Nichū school, formed during the period of this study, was not included under the generic PTA mantle. The purpose of the organization was to honor a local Uena region boy who had become a professional baseball star on one of Japan's major teams. It was another *kōenkai* (supporters' organization), but not specifically for the support of the school. Rather, it was an attempt to honor the hometown boy who had "made good," and, in so doing, to show the pride of the local community.

The honored baseball player was a graduate of the postwar school system, including both Nichū and the adjacent Ichikō High School. The idea of the organization and its first backers came from the Ichikō High School's local alumni organization and included many who already held office in the Nichū PTA. However, it was felt that many people interested in the baseball player's career would not be included if the Ichikō alumni organization alone sponsored the *kōenkai*. Therefore, a separate and wider organization was proposed.

An organizational meeting was called during the period of winter vacation in the schools. Nichū teachers were informed of the meeting by the head teacher. Little doubt was left that participation was mandatory for teachers. The baseball star was an honor to Nichū and the teachers would, accordingly, have to participate in the honoring organization. The first meeting was held in the auditorium of the Ichikō High School, where the Nichū principal was able to publicly announce 100 percent participation by his teaching staff. For some, this included payment of dues while they "forgot" about attending the formal meeting.

At that first meeting, a formal set of organizational by-laws was adopted and officers selected. The Nichū PTA chairman was unanimously elected president of the new organization, while the Tokai Town representative to the Nippon City Board of Education became one of three vice-chairmen. The PTA chairman was chosen because, in the words of one of the group's new leaders, "he is a man of great character in these parts." The chairman was not, however, a member of the Ichikō alumni group that originally proposed the organization.

In these circumstances, the Nichū school had a clear responsibility to the community to participate actively in the formation of the new organization. Both the principal and the head teacher were in the group of active organizers, and they made sure that all Nichū teachers were involved.

In any modern society, the examination of local forms of interaction between the school and its community is insufficient. The school is not only a part of the local community and local school system, but it is also socially and administratively integrated with the larger regional and national society. The following chapter begins a description of the ways in which Nichū School is an integral part of the larger city, prefectural, and national system of education.

6 / School and administration interaction

I N JAPAN, local and prefectural boards of education act as administrative extensions of the Ministry of Education. Technically independent, the actual boards are appointed by local and prefectural political authorities and act as advisory committees to the legislative councils. Professional administrative personnel in the offices attached to local and prefectural boards appear to be representatives of the Ministry of Education, as well as of the local boards.

Local autonomy for Japanese municipalities and prefectures was one of the major goals of the American Occupation. This goal was implemented by the Local Autonomy Law of 1947 which aimed "to decentralize administration in order to prevent any re-emergence of the totalitarian central control which had characterized the prewar Japan" (Dore 1959:318–319). The establishment of local boards of education in Japan in 1948, a move initiated by the American Occupation, was intended to provide a structure for local control of education in the American pattern. The Ministry of Education says that, "national and local agencies operate cooperatively, though national agencies have no administrative control over local agencies except in special instances" (1961:31).

However, there are many factors in the Japanese situation that tend to negate the independence and autonomy of local boards of education. They are largely the same factors which limit local autonomy for all agencies of Japanese local government. Dore has described three such major factors. First, national legislation limits closely the scope of discretion allowed to local agencies. Secondly, the traditional reliance on authority dies hard. "The Minister of Education's powers to offer 'guidance, advice, and assistance' to local education committees are exercised in a constant stream of memoranda, outline curricula, and model sets of regulations, and these tend to carry an authority not very different from that of the directives and regulations of prewar days." Thirdly, the local agencies lack financial autonomy (1959:320). A board of education does not have its own tax base, but is dependent on municipal and prefectural assemblies for budget appropriations.

All public school teachers from the elementary school through the high school are employees of the prefecture and receive their pay and school assignments from the prefectural education office. A few exceptions occur when teachers are hired directly by a school or local board for special purposes, usually without holding regular teaching certificates. There were no Nichū teachers in this category. Ultimate authority for the transfer or promotion of teachers rests with the prefectural office.

Third-year Nichū pupils taking the national achievement examinations.

Assignments of teachers to schools and annual inspections of the school are carried out by prefectural office representatives.

While the Ministry of Education stands at the apex of the administrative pyramid over Nichū, it is not a large organization in terms of the number of people employed. Total personnel of the Ministry of Education in 1961 was 1166 (Ministry of Education 1961:33). Only 215 of these people are in the Department of Elementary and Secondary Education, including 11 supervisors and 29 curriculum specialists. Obviously, the Ministry is in no position to supervise directly the 26,858 elementary schools, 12,986 middle schools, 5,937 full-time and part-time high schools, and other public and private educational institutions (Ministry of Education 1961:50).

The Ministry of Education had, in 1962, twelve national inspectors who were subject matter specialists having responsibility for geographical regions in Japan. They worked mostly with prefectural education offices, but sometimes had direct contact with local boards of education.

Centralized control of education, therefore, comes not from the direct personal supervision of schools by Ministry of Education officialdom, but rather from the supervision of lower levels of administrative superstructure combined with impersonal forces controlled by the ministry. It is the ministry, at the national level, which issues the national curricula for public and private schools, approves all school textbooks, administers a standardized nationwide achievement test at several grade levels, establishes national standards and procedures for school administration, passes out substantial subsidy funds for approved projects, and initiates in-service training projects to meet national goals.

One of the newer forms of direct control over the local school by the Ministry of

Education is the administration of the national achievement examinations in all middle schools. The first compulsory nationwide tests were given in 1961. At that time, there was strong opposition to the tests by the Japan Teachers Union and many demonstrations by teachers and others were organized to upset the Ministry's plans for the tests. These occurred mainly in areas known for the strength of their local teachers' union. The newspapers and television reports of the examinations emphasized the opposition to the tests, but in reality, most schools, including Nichū, administered the examinations without question.

The second round of national achievement examinations were given in July, 1962, and were again opposed by the Japan Teachers Union. However, the opposition movements were smaller and even less effective than those that occurred during the first test. Nichū school teachers were not involved in demonstrations of opposition beyond the signing of a union-sponsored anti-achievement test petition.

The prefectural education office has some channels of direct control over Nichū. Teachers are prefectural employees and their salary comes from the prefectural administration, though half the cost of salaries is borne by the national government. Public school administration, that is, certification, recruitment, placement, transfer, and promotion of school personnel, is the responsibility of the prefecture. The only direct employees of the Nippon City Board of Education are the people who work in its administrative office or staff educational programs outside the elmentary-secondary main-line of public school education. One kindergarten is operated as a municipal school and the teachers are direct employees of the Board of Education. The local board has no connection with the high schools located in Nippon City. These high schools are controlled directly by the prefectural Board of Education.

Actual supervision of the Nichū Middle School in the implementation of the national objectives, as stated by the Ministry, is the responsibility of both the local and prefectural boards of education.

The Nippon City Board of Education, composed of five men appointed by the mayor of Nippon City and approved by the City Assembly, meets once a month to discuss educational policy, but has no direct control over the administration of education in the city. It does present a recommended education budget to the Mayor and City Assembly each year, but one Nippon City board member intimated that the heaviest responsibility related to the budget was to persuade the City Assembly to appropriate the money requested.

Of the five members of the board, two were retired school principals, one was a wealthy, elderly farmer, one a doctor, and one the local city superintendent of education. The local superintendent is a full member of the Board of Education. The Nippon City superintendent came to this present job after being director of research for the prefectural education office. The board chairman was one of the retired school principals who had difficulty getting around in his declining years. Only the doctor and superintendent were too young to qualify for retirement.

Most directly involved in the supervision of Nichū were the three *shidō shuji* employed by the Nippon City Board of Education. These men acted as supervisors and teacher-consultants in the city's elementary and middle schools. All three were experienced teachers who had been employed in the Nippon City schools before promotion to their *shidō shuji* positions. As such, they were direct employees of the city's board of education.

Though "teacher-consultant" is the English translation used by the Ministry of Education for *shidō shuji,* emphasizing the connection with modern American concepts of school administration introduced by the American Occupation authorities, it is difficult to completely avoid the translation "supervisor" when one observes the activities and responsibilities of these men. The supervisory relationship fits much more clearly into the tradition of Japanese educational and governmental administration. When the national achievement test was being administered in the middle schools by order of the Ministry of Education, for instance, it was a city *shidō shuji* who came to Nichū to see if the instructions for administration of the examination were being properly carried out.

Nippon City was one of the three cities in its prefecture which hired *shidō shuji* directly to work for the local boards of education. In other cities, towns, and villages, the only *shidō shuji* working with the schools were those attached to regional offices of the prefectural Board of Education.

In practice, with relation to the Nippon City schools, the prefectural and city *shidō shuji* worked closely together in their supervision of and assistance to teachers.

The Nippon City Board of Education *shidō shuji* maintained friendly relations with the Nichū teachers. They were regularly invited to participate in special Nichū activities. On the occasion of a party sponsored by Nichū for the teachers of Nichū and the two elementary schools in its district to become acquainted, one of the city *shidō shuji* came to participate.

FORMAL SCHOOL VISITS

Each school in Nippon City was scheduled for a formal visit once a year by a team of *shidō shuji* representing each level of educational administration in the prefecture. The dates of these formal visits were set well in advance at a time suggested by the schools concerned. They were a time for formal consultation and supervision at the schools.

Ten days before the scheduled visit to Nichū, the faculty steering committee met in the principal's office to make specific plans for the occasion. Following a common pattern, the morning was set aside for class observation by the visiting *shidō shuji*. At noon, the pupils were to be dismissed with the afternoon being reserved for a conference of the teachers and *shidō shuji*. Subjects which the steering committee decided to emphasize were morals education, homeroom guidance, club activities, and English and vocational subjects.

At the teachers' meeting two days later, the plans of the steering committee were discussed without any evidence of anxiety on the part of the teachers or principal. The normal class schedule for the day of the general visit was discarded. Instead, the teachers arranged among themselves an equitable schedule of classes and subjects, there was some trading and shifting of classes to accommodate individual preferences. Though the meeting lasted much longer than usual, the only other accomplishment, aside from the scheduling of classes for the coming visit, were the plans made for advance printing of the lesson plans in a booklet to be presented to the *shidō shuji.*

Before the day of the visit, there was a general clean-up of the school and its grounds by both pupils and teachers. The day before, programs listing the names of the visiting *shidō shuji,* the schedule of activities, and individual lesson plans for each demonstration class were passed out to the teachers. Besides the three city *shidō shuji,* there were three from the prefectural office, who arrived at Nichū before the beginning of classes on the appointed day. They were entertained by the principal in his office while the teachers held their regular morning meeting with the head teacher. They appeared calm about the procedure. Once the chimes were rung, announcing the beginning of the first class, the five *shidō shuji* spread out through the school visiting classes individually or in pairs. Typically, they would enter the class by a rear door, study the notices that were on the blackboards or posted on the bulletin board, look closely at their program descriptions of the teacher's lesson plan, peer over the shoulders of a few pupils to see what they were writing in their notebooks, and listen for a short time to the teacher. They wrote notes on their programs about each class and left without any formal acknowledgement of their presence by the teacher or class.

Before the chimes had rung, indicating the end of a class period, the *shidō shuji* returned to the principal's office to sit and wait for the beginning of the next class. Each visitor covered all the classes in a single hour. There was no attempt to divide up responsibility for coverage.

During the fourth and final period of the morning, the pupils assembled for their club activities—the sports and special interest club groups that met regularly once a week. One of the city *shidō shuji* had made preliminary arrangements with the teacher responsible for the *kendō* (Japanese fencing) club. He joined in the students' activity, having brought along his personal equipment. He was the only visitor to join in the pupils' activities of the day. Later, in the group meeting with the teachers, he referred to this participation in commenting that the Nichū pupils seemed especially gentle and obedient but were, perhaps, not lively enough. The comment reflected a community stereotype of Nichū which had been expressed to the author by parents and teachers before, and was generally attributed to the traditional nature of the school district.

Though only about two thirds of the teachers were teaching in any one period, there was no visiting of classes by the free teachers. They restricted themselves to the teachers room when not teaching, as usual, and the principal and the author were the only people, in addition to the *shidō shuji,* observing the classes in action. This was the only time that Nichū teachers organized small, group discussions and activities in their classes—a favorite demonstration technique for in-service training programs.

The visitors were given special lunches in the principal's office before coming together with the teachers in the music room for a general discussion meeting. The principal opened the meeting and then turned it over to two senior Nichū teachers who had prepared special speeches for the occasion that concerned the programs of morals education and guidance that had been worked out for Nichū.

Next, each *shidō shuji* presented his own comments. Each gave positive expressions of opinion about the Nichū school program, but several made specific criticisms of classes that they had visited. One of the prefectural office representatives clearly assumed the role of teacher during this meeting. He had several standard lists of points which he wanted to make about specific subject classes. When he came to one of these lists, he would repeat each statement slowly and leave enough time for the teachers to copy it exactly into their notebooks. Dutifully, the teachers did as expected and gave every indication of careful attention to the rather long and rambling lecture.

By the time that the last speaker, the senior representative of the prefectural education office, rose to speak, the meeting had lasted three hours. Few teachers were taking notes as industriously as they had at the beginning. Those sitting in front of the author were doodling in their books rather than taking notes.

When the meeting was finally closed by the principal, teachers and visitors went to another classroom where the tables had been set for a party. The *sashimi* (raw fish) and pork cutlets had been prepared by the school cook and the tables were well loaded with *sake*. After the formal opening by the principal and the drinking of the first round of *sake,* the party proceeded. Like other such parties that the author observed, the purpose (and actual result) was to make the participants more intimate and friendly with each other. The principal and several of the visitors took care to exchange thimble-sized cups of *sake* with the teachers as well as engage all others who were present in this friendly ritual.

The teachers had shown few signs of specific concern or anxiety about the procedures involved, either in preparation for the general visit, participation in the activities of the day, or in the final party.

DESIGNATION OF EXPERIMENTAL SCHOOL

Not all attempts by the *shidō shuji* to supervise and direct educational activities at Nichū were as successful with the teachers. Illustrative of the relations of Nichū and the local board of education was the manner in which the Nichū school received notice that it was designated as the city's experimental school for morals education. About a month after the opening of the school year, the three city *shidō shuji* came to a special afternoon teachers' meeting at Nichū. The teachers had no prior hint of the purpose of their visit. Sitting quietly in the teachers' office, looking down at their desks rather than at the speaker who sat at the head of the room, they listened as the three *shidō shuji* talked in turn and relayed the news that Nichū had been selected by the board of education to carry out a three-year experimental program in morals education.

The practice of rotating experimental school designations in the city had been in effect for some time. In general, the five middle schools took their turns. Vocational education and international education had been the research subjects for other middle schools in preceding years. In some cases, special, national or prefectural subsidies had been used by the experimental schools to carry out new educational programs.

The three *shidō shuji* explained to the Nichū teachers that the question of morals education was very timely and had been picked as appropriate for emphasis by Nichū. Included in the short talks by the consultants were references to the new national curriculum, the national reintroduction of morals as a school subject in the elementary and middle schools, the necessity for thinking of "life guidance" in connection with morals education, and a brief reminder of the national achievement examinations for middle school pupils that were to be given later in the year.

The Nichū principal was the only member of the Nichū staff who had been given prior notice of the selection of the school for these purposes. Apparently, he had not communicated this news to the teachers in advance of the meeting with the *shidō shuji*.

When the *shidō shuji* had finished their half-hour presentation to the teachers, the meeting was called to a close. No teacher had spoken or asked a question during the presentation, nor was any indication given that they were expected to participate in a discussion. The *shidō shuji* accompanied the principal to his room, leaving the teachers to carry on with their desk work. One of the consultants, however, came back to the teachers' room shortly after and joked in a friendly manner with two of the older teachers. No other teachers came up to talk with them.

In private conversations later, the teachers indicated resentment that they had not been consulted in the choice of the research topic they were asked to pursue. Most of them felt that the principal had erred in allowing the board of education to reach a decision without first notifying or consulting with them that the subject was under consideration. The teachers expected to be a party to any decisions that were made on research topics for their school. They did, however, accept the inevitable designation of Nichū as an experimental school.

During the two months following the original announcement by the *shidō shuji*, the author sat on the fringes of five teachers' meetings that were devoted to the question of a research topic that would be acceptable to the Nichū teachers. One senior teacher objected specifically to the choice of morals education as a research topic. He wanted some other subject.

That the teachers must reach a consensus on the research topic for Nichū was an unquestioned assumption of the ensuing discussions. No one, in any of the meetings, called for a vote to resolve the issue. Instead, those who were trying to expedite a decision urged the others to speak up with their views. Several times the suggestion was made that the teachers be called on in turn to express their feelings. At first this suggestion was resisted on the grounds that it was a childish way to proceed. Later, however, the suggestion was accepted, and the teachers, especially the younger ones, were called on to express their views directly. At the last meeting before the summer vacation period, a mimeographed proposal for morals education research was passed out to the teachers, but there was still some uncertainty about the nature of the decision that had been reached.

During the course of the meetings, a shifting pattern in the leadership of the discussion occurred. After the second meeting, the principal became a quiet ob-

server, giving up the direction of the meetings as formal chairman, and participating verbally only to the extent that he would answer questions directed to him.
The head teacher, too, assumed a passive role, though he spoke more often than the
principal. Several teachers took over discussion leadership in the teachers' meetings
to assist in arriving at a consensus. The first teacher to take over discussion leadership, Mr. Hagida, did so with no apparent preconceived plan and without being
formally designated. A jovial science teacher who had been a classmate of the principal in the prefectural normal school before the war, he tried to push the teachers
from their "silent resistance" to acquiescence with the decision of the Board of
Education. This was interpreted by a young teacher as an attempt to help his
friend, the principal, out of a difficult position.

To do this, Mr. Hagida first took an active part in the discussion by emphasizing
the need for a decision by the teachers. Then he proposed that the meeting be concluded in half an hour, pulling his chair to the front of the room where he could
sit behind the principal's desk and direct the proceedings. Though unable to get a
consensus within his time limit, he proposed to the principal that the meetings be
extended for another day. The principal assented reluctantly.

In the next meeting, Mr. Hagida opened the discussion by moving to the principal's desk and acting as a formal chairman. Before the end of this second meeting,
he retreated back to his desk, unable to overcome the "silent resistance" to a consensus. Before the end of the meeting, another of the older teachers assumed control and proposed that a five-man committee be appointed by the teachers to make
definite proposals. This was generally accepted and carried out.

The next meeting was presided over by a younger teacher who was asked to assume the role of chairman. At first he seemed embarrassed and reluctant to take
over the meeting. Once in position at the head of the room, however, he exercised
rather firm control over the discussion including admonitions to teachers who tended
to monopolize the discussion. First, he called on four teachers who gave formal
presentations of their proposals. Each of them spoke for ten minutes to half an
hour from previously prepared notes. The research subjects thus formally presented
were:

(1) Morals education
(2) Student government activities
(3) Student club activities
(4) Class activities

Several of the teachers in their discussion occasionally tried to propose individual-
ized research programs rather than a unified topic for all, but this did not appear to
be an acceptable alternative. In spite of the presentation of alternative proposals for
a research theme by the teachers, the discussions eventually led to the apparently
inescapable conclusion that Nichū was to become an experimental school for
morals education.

On November 1, six months after the initial proposal by the *shidō shuji*, a committee of teachers met to lay specific plans for the research project on morals education. Once designated as a research topic, the teachers were left to carry the responsibility. The *shidō shuji* were to be available for advice upon request.

Possibly, the party arranged at the conclusion of the "general visit' by the *shidō shuji* was designed by the Nichū principal for the sole purpose of reestablishing good relationships between the teachers and the local *shidō shuji.*

Most of the teachers felt that the principal had erred in not discussing the research topic with his staff before the formal announcement, hence, they continued their "silent resistance." In spite of opposition from the Japan Teachers Union to the teaching of morals education as a separate subject, none of the Nichū teachers took this position. They all agreed to the importance of morals education as a subject in itself. Their protest was against the principal for having acted as an agent of the board of education rather than as a mediator between the teachers and the board of education. If they had been consulted earlier by the principal, their major complaint would have been resolved.

Six months after the first announcement by the city *shidō shuji* of the morals education experimental school plan, the teachers had worked out a tentative research plan and were committed to the project. A steering committee had been formed and the first demonstration class in morals education had been planned.

IN-SERVICE EDUCATION AND PROFESSIONAL MEETINGS

A particularly striking characteristic of Japanese schools, for an American observer, is the large number of meetings devoted to teachers' professional study, research, and training. Almost every Monday, when the Nichū head teacher wrote the weekly schedule of special activities on the blackboard at the head of the teachers' room, there would be an announcement of one or more special meetings of teachers to be held at one of the Nippon City schools, at the prefectural capital, or elsewhere. For each of these meetings, one or more teachers would be delegated to attend as a Nichū representative. These meetings were generally sponsored by one of the administrative offices concerned with education, other local government offices, some part of the teachers union, or one of the local schools.

Such professional meetings represented one of the major areas of teacher interaction with the administrative community, a place where the administrators had a chance to influence the teachers and *vice-versa.*

Four major types of professional meetings were sponsored by administrative agencies: (1) orientation meetings to explain new programs or curriculum changes being introduced by the Ministry of Education, (2) demonstration meetings of model school or experimental school curriculum and research activities, (3) specialty meetings of subject-matter teachers or specialists for the exchange of ideas and information, and (4) institutes or short courses for teachers in teaching methods or subject content.

Having described the administrative integration of Nichū School with the national system of Japanese education, it is now important to describe its relation to and interaction with the other major national force in education, the Japan Teachers Union and the professional community of teachers which it represents.

7 / School and teachers union interaction

JUST AS THE Japan Teachers Union (JTU) includes about 90 percent of Japanese elementary and middle school teachers in its organization, so does it encompass many of the professional activities of teachers. Other than the governmental administrative organizations and their programs which have just been described, the JTU and related teachers union activities account for the greatest part of the professional activity of Japanese teachers.

It is, perhaps, a unique feature of Japanese education that there is a clearly separable administrative and professional community in direct contact with the schools. Though there are many professional activities carried out under the auspices of the administrative community, the teachers union is a clearly separate entity with which the teachers are identified and within which there is a good deal of professional as well as union activity. Partly due to the national controversy between the JTU and the Ministry of Education, there is usually a clear distinction between union-related and professional administrative activities. This is true, even in the prefecture of Nichū, where there is a unique practice of combining administrative support with one union-sponsored activity, the annual educational research meeting.

The JTU is organized with four levels of union associations. At the top, there is the *Nippon Kyōshokuin Kumiai* (Japan Teachers Union) which is usually called *Nikkyōso*. The executive offices of the national JTU are located in Tokyo in an old brick building called the *Kyōikukaikan* (education hall). Five stories high, it is usually draped with one or more long white streamers on which are printed the union's current slogans. Also located in the building are the offices of the high school teachers union which is a separate and weaker union whose membership includes only about one third of all high school teachers.

A weekly newspaper and a monthly journal published by the central office are used for direct communication with the JTU membership. At Nichū school, these periodicals came directly to the school and were available in the teachers' room.

An annual nationwide educational research meeting for teacher members is sponsored by the JTU and always receives much attention. The Ministry of Education began, during the period of this study, to sponsor a smaller competitive research meeting for teachers.

The JTU finances its own research organization, the Peoples Education Research Institute, which publishes regular reports of its own educational research in a variety of forms. As might be expected, the problems chosen for study are generally within the area of union concern. The Ministry of Education finances a National Institute of Educational Research, in addition to its own research section. Thus the Ministry and the JTU have parallel and competitive research organizations.

During the period of this study, no Nichū teacher was observed to have had direct personal contact with the central JTU office. It is likely, however, that some teachers went to meetings where national JTU officers were present.

The second level of JTU organization consists of the prefectural unions. Each prefecture has its own union organization with a headquarters staff maintaining union affairs. The relative strength or enthusiasm of the prefectural unions varies greatly and seems to be related to a number of factors. Tokyo, a prefecture in itself, has one of the strongest union organizations. Seevral outlying rural prefectures also have the reputation of being especially strong in union support.

The prefecture which included Nippon City, however, was known for the weak union spirit of its teachers. During the period of this study, no major teachers union demonstration was observed in the prefecture or recorded in the local newspapers; though demonstrations and activities elsewhere were noted.

The prefectural teachers union had its central office in the capital city of the prefecture about three blocks from the prefectural Board of Education office. Located in a small, two-story "education hall" which it shared with the high school teachers union, a full-time executive staff ran the affairs of the union's prefectural branch.

The current chairman of the prefectural union had formerly been principal of a large elementary school. The vice-chairman had come from his job as head teacher of an elementary school. One of the other prefectural officers had been a head teacher before election to his current job. However, it was indicated that the number of principals and head teachers entering prefectural union offices in recent years had declined.

At the time of this study, there were several features of prefectural teachers union organizations that varied from one prefecture to the next. One was the degree of participation by principals and head teachers in union affairs. In the Tokyo teachers union, for instance, principals and head teachers no longer participated. In the prefecture concerned in this study, principals and head teachers were still active participants in union affairs. The question of whether they could or should continue this role in union affairs was under active discussion. The Ministry of Education was applying pressure to the school administrators to leave the union.

A second differentiating feature of prefectural teachers union organization was the occurrence in some prefectures of two separate organizations, one representing the JTU and the other carrying on as a prefectural teachers union. Such a separation of offices was not established in Nichū's prefecture. The union officials interviewed by the author were careful to explain their feeling of complete support for the JTU and would not indicate any areas of possible conflict between local and national goals.

Third, some prefectures were able to support full-time employees at local branch offices of the teachers union. In this prefecture, there were no such employees, or local branch offices, though one prefecture visited by the author has an "education hall" and local office in each region.

The next level of teachers union organization is called the *shibu* (local branch). In the prefecture of Nichū there were more than twenty *shibu* organized on a regional basis that covered the prefecture completely. Nichū school was included in the Nippon City *shibu*. Though each *shibu* had a formal organization, specialized sections, and a regular program of meetings, it had no physical office facilities in this prefecture.

Once a year, each *shibu* would hold a general membership meeting with elections of local officials. The executive committee of the *shibu* would meet monthly to carry out the business of the union.

Important sections of the *shibu* which maintained their own slate of officers and program of meetings in addition to the regular *shibu* activities were the women's division, the youth division, and the school clerks' division. All female teachers were members of the women's division and all male teachers less than thirty-five years old were included in the youth division. The school clerks, though union members, did not participate in the *shibu* general meeting. Rather, the school clerks held an annual prefecture-wide meeting.

Principals and head teachers monopolized the top elective positions in the different *shibu* of Nichū's prefecture. Only one *shibu* chairman was not a school principal. In Nippon City, an elementary school principal was elected chairman during the period of this study, replacing a middle school principal in the job.

Both the principal and the head teacher of Nichū had served in various union offices, though they were not holding a union office during the period of this study. When the author first questioned a Nichū teacher-representative to the general committee of the *shibu* about the way to arrange for observation of the meeting, he was referred to the Nichū head teacher and principal. Though they indicated some initial reluctance, the principal tried to resolve the question by a direct phone call to the *shibu* chairman. When he found that the chairman was out of town, he took it upon himself to issue an invitation to the meeting, after a short consultation with some of the teachers. He explained, "Last year it would have been a problem, but this year it should be all right. The Nippon City teachers union is weak. The principals and head teachers are included here—but that is a problem, too."

A fourth level of union organization was the *bunkai* (chapter) which included all teachers in one school. Each *bunkai* was expected to elect representatives to the *shibu* general committee and the *shibu* executive comittee. The executive committee representative was most important because he formed the major communication link between the teachers and the union organization.

ANNUAL MEETING OF THE NIPPON CITY *SHIBU*

On the first Saturday in June, shortly after the opening of the school year, the annual meeting of the Nippon City branch of the prefectural teachers union was scheduled. The mimeographed program describing the order and content of business indicated that the meeting was planned to last from one-thirty to five o'clock in the afternoon. In this manner, the meeting did not infringe upon the official forty-four hours, five-and-a-half day working week of the teachers. It was the only meeting of any kind during the year at which all of the Nippon City teachers were expected to assemble. Of 403 members of the *shibu,* the official attendance count showed 268 actually present with eighty proxies received. This allowed the meeting to fulfill the union requirement that two thirds of the membership must be present (physically or by proxy) to constitute an official quorum for the conduct of union business.

The meeting was held in a centrally-located Nippon City elementary school assembly hall. In attendance, as invited guests, in addition to the teachers and a curious American researcher, were the vice-chairman of the prefectural teachers union, a Socialist member of the Nippon City Assembly, and the Nippon City superintendent of education. None of the city or prefectural *shidō shuji* were at the meeting. The teachers sat in sections of the assembly hall assigned to their school. Union officials and committee members sat on the stage in front of the hall. The three invited guests sat at a table at one side of the front of the hall.

As the meeting opened, three men were chosen, ostensibly without prior notice, to chair the meeting in rotation. The Nichū head teacher was the first one so chosen and left his seat in the Nichū section of the hall to take over the meeting. He called the meeting to order and the chairman from the previous year, principal of the Nippon City Yonchū Middle School, gave his opening greetings. He mentioned several union problems of national scope, among which were the nationwide achievement testing program being carried out by the Ministry of Education and the question of inclusion of principals in the union. The chairman's short talk was followed by an introduction of new teachers in each of the schools represented. This completed the opening formalities of the meeting.

First on the agenda was a report of the previous year's activities of the *shibu.* Some time was spent describing the problems that arose out of the transfer to another school, without prior consultation or notice, of two Tokai Elementary School teachers. Union activists with the local reputation of being Communists, they had protested their transfer publicly at the previous annual meeting of the *shibu.* Their case had been taken to court by the union. In spite of this action, the two teachers had not been returned to the Tokai school.

Descriptions of the struggles against the merit rating system for teachers, the nationwide achievement examinations, and the present salary scale for teachers formed the body of the report. The concluding statement described the research reports and activities of the *shibu,* some of which had been included in the national JTU-sponsored research meeting.

Questions from the floor were related to the achievement testing problem. One teacher wanted to know how long the local board of education's promise would hold to not use the test results in evaluation of teachers. Another added his doubts about the construction of the tests.

The official program for the coming year, given in a series of five slogans, was then proposed. Mild applause was the signal for approval of the program as stated.

No opposition was expressed to the slogans which represented the major concerns of the JTU in the political and economic sphere.

One young teacher rose from the floor of the meeting to propose a resolution, addressed to the Nippon City Assembly opposing the scheduled installation of a missile-launching base near Nippon City. The presiding officer ruled him out-of-order because he had not brought up his proposal before the opening of the business session. The *shibu* chairman, however, intervened to propose that a vote be taken on whether the proposed resolution should be discussed at the meeting. The chairman asked, "Who is against discussion of this problem?" When only two people stood up to signify their opposition, the discussion began. After some confused parliamentary procedure, mild applause signaled the passing of the resolution.

An older Nichū teacher said later that he did not feel the resolution represented the feelings of the majority of the teachers. He attributed its passage to a few "young red hot-heads." He felt that the older teachers really agreed with the national government on this issue.

A good deal of time was taken up on budgetary reports and proposals. When the officers proposed an increase in *shibu* dues, two men and a woman stood up to say why they approved of the increase. A Nichū teacher commented fatalistically, "It is gradually getting more difficult to express any opposition." As before, mild applause was used to signal approval of the proposed budget, including the raise in dues.

An important item of business that raised a good deal of discussion was a proposed revision of the *shibu* constitution. The major effect of the revision was to change the system of election of *shibu* officers so that they might be elected earlier in the year at local school *bunkai* meetings, rather than waiting for the annual general meeting. Several younger teachers expressed vehement opposition to the proposed revision. One of them, a teacher involved in the previous year's personnel transfer problem previously described, complained that the principals would be able to dominate the elections if they were held in the local schools. Only at the general meeting did he feel free of the influence of his principal. The statements of the younger teachers in opposition were vehement and vigorous. Occasionally, one of them would call out *dōkan* (expression of approval) loudly at one of the other teachers' points. But the majority of teachers remained uninvolved in the discussion. One elementary school principal did stand up to express his opinion that the *hantai* (opposition) arguments were "feeble."

Then the chairman requested that speakers in favor of revision make their views known. Three teachers, in turn, were ruled out of order when they rose to express more opposition arguments.

Finally a vote was called for on the revision of the constitution. For the first time, hands were raised to cast a vote and the votes were counted carefully. The results of the vote were not clear and seemed ambiguous. The chairman called for a second vote, but was vigorously opposed by the younger teachers. The chairman had to retract his proposal for a recount and announced that although a majority of those present had voted in favor of the revision, the necessary two-thirds vote for a constitutional revision had not been reached. Thus the small group of young radical teachers, as they were generally regarded, won a small victory in the meeting.

When it came time to vote for the next year's officers, an elaborate ballot box and voting booth apparatus was erected on the stage in front of the hall. The teachers lined up and had their names checked as they received a ballot. Despite the physical trappings, however, they had only one slate of nominated officers from which to choose. Their vote was merely a "yes" or "no" in the case of each candidate selected by the nominating committee. A good deal of time was taken up with the voting and the counting of ballots after the ballots had been marked. John B. Cornell, an anthropologist who studied a *buraku* election of local officials in a rural community, noted a similar type of process. "The formal selection, though done by ballot, is merely part of the form that since the war has come to be regarded as democratic procedure" (1962:38).

A Nichū teacher later told the author that it was not always the case, however, that there was a single slate of nominees on the ballot for union officials. The previous year, one of the young teachers involved in the school transfer problem mentioned above, had opposed the Yonchū principal in the election and had drawn quite a few votes.

During the ballot-counting, the vice-chairman of the prefectural teachers union was called on for a speech. He presented two proposals to the teachers, one related to a union mutual aid fund and the other to the disposition of money awarded to the teachers for back pay which had been secured by a union court action. In each case he received informal approval by the meeting without discussion. He then spoke of the different national JTU struggles. Immediately following his speech, the Nippon City superintendent of education was called on to give his greetings. He spoke in general terms for a brief ten minutes.

It was then the turn of the Socialist City Assembly member to talk to the group. He ranged over a variety of political questions and included some references to the coming Diet election. His electioneering caused some amusement among the teachers.

After some time, the ballots were counted and the results announced. The slate of officers nominated had been accepted. There was a short speech from the new *shibu* chairman and concluding greetings from the outgoing chairman and vice-chairman before the meeting finally came to a close, later than the previously-announced closing hour.

By comparison with the public clamor on the national level between the JTU and the Ministry of Education, the *shibu* meeting was meek and gentle. There had been perfunctory approval of slogans supporting the national JTU platform. One political issue had been raised relating to the missile base installations in Nippon City. The inclusion in the union activities of principals and the invitation to the city superintendent of education to the meeting gave an appearance of professional more than trade union organization. The discussion relating to the proposed revision of the *shibu* constitution was the single incident that cast a union-orientation into the meeting. During the discussion the idea was expressed that principals and teachers were representing opposing sides in a labor-management model of school organization. Such feelings were evidently held by a minority of the teachers at the meeting, though they were able to block the proposed constitutional changes.

SHIBU COMMITTEES AND SECTIONS

Two *shibu* committees have already been mentioned. The general committee is composed of representatives from each *bunkai,* with the number of representatives being proportional to the number of teachers in the *bunkai,* on the basis of one representative for every ten teachers. This makes a total of forty-three representatives on the general committee, including two representatives from each of the two *shibu* section organizations described below. This committee met rarely. Some announcements generated by meetings of the general committee were made during Nichū daily teachers' meeting periods.

The second committee, called the executive committee, has one representative from each *bunkai* and section and includes the elected officers of the *shibu*. It meets monthly and is responsible for carrying on the business of the *shibu* between the annual meetings. The executive committee is particularly responsible for communication from the higher levels of union organization to the teachers and for the organization of activities initiated either locally or from above. At Nichū during the daily teachers' meetings before school, the executive committee representative would occasionally announce the decisions of the committee and carry out union-initiated activities.

The first meeting of both the executive and general committees was combined. It occurred six days after the general meeting of the *shibu.* Major items of business included the selection of twenty Nippon City representatatives to the general meeting of prefectural teachers union scheduled for the following week, and representatives for standing committees of the prefectural union.

One of the activities carried out by the executive committee during the period of this study was a conference of union representatives with the Nippon City superintendent of education. The meeting was requested by the union for the purpose of protesting against the nationwide achievement testing program of the Ministry. They secured a promise from the superintendent that the test results would not be used for the evaluation of teachers, which was the committee's major concern.

Two sections of the *shibu* cut across *bunkai* divisions to enlist all the women teachers in the women's section and all of the male teachers under thirty-five years of age in the youth section. These sections maintained separate organizations and held annual meetings as well as sponsoring some special activities. These sections were affiliated, in turn, with the women's and youth sections of the prefectural teachers' union.

Female teachers at Nichū were not especially active in the Nippon City *shibu* women's section. The youngest Nichū teacher, a home economics specialist, was the Nichū representative to the committee of the women's section which met on a monthly basis. Like the *shibu,* itself, there was an annual meeting for all the female teachers and a committee to carry on the affairs of the section at another time. One of the older Nichū female teachers described the activities, other than the annual meeting, as including institutes for the study of laws relating to women's rights as teachers and workers, sessions for cooking and sewing lessons, and the promotion of meetings bringing mothers and female teachers together for discussion of educational problems.

The youth section of the *shibu* had a local reputation of being the most radical and active of the teachers union activities. This was, in part, a reflection of the national reputation of the younger teachers in the union.

Several of the Nichū teachers were active in the youth section. During the annual meeting, a radical leadership group was deposed from power in favor of a more moderate group.

Organized like the *shibu* and the women's section, the annual meeting was a time for business relating to the program for the year and the election of officers. About one hundred and twenty teachers came to meet in the cramped library of the Itchū Middle School on a Thursday afternoon about four weeks after the *shibu's* annual meeting. Two older officers of the *shibu,* formerly active in the youth section, attended as observers for the *shibu.*

Less formally organized than the *shibu's* annual meeting, the program was similar. Reports of past and proposed activities, finances, and slogans were much the same. In the mimeographed program, activities of the past year were listed under five sections: (1) protection of peace, independence, and democracy, (2) protection of democratic education, (3) protection of livelihood and rights, (4) enlargement of freedom for union activities, and (5) miscellaneous.

Under the first section, stress was laid on activities of youth division members in the anti-atomic bomb testing movement. "Protection of democratic action" had been supported by opposition to the nationwide achievement tests and participation in regional research and study meetings.

In his concluding remarks on activities of the past year, the chairman was critical of teacher participation in youth division activities. He felt that the meetings of the general committee had been very poor, and that the youth division programs were insufficiently active. He blamed this on the fact that members were so busy in their work as teachers and in carrying out their school responsibilities. He also mentioned, though, a lack of spirit among the members of the youth section's committee and a lack of spirited guidance from the youth division officers. These comments reflected his own position as a union activist.

When the time came for election of new officers, there was, again, a single slate of nominees. The same collapsible ballot box and voting booths that had been set up for the *shibu* general meeting were used and the teachers lined up to cast their ballots.

The election results that were announced indicated, however, that the entire slate of officers had been rejected. This left the chairman obviously confused on how to proceed. Since it was already past the scheduled closing time of the meeting, someone suggested that it be adjourned. Another person suggested that a committee be appointed to nominate a new slate of officers. Amidst some confusion, such a committee was appointed and it retired from the room to consider the problem. After some time during which there was no programed activity for the general meeting, the committee returned to announce its nominations. Instead of going through the balloting procedure once more, the new slate of officers was elected by acclamation and the meeting adjourned after a brief greeting from the new chairman.

Until this meeting, the leadership of the youth section had been dominated by representatives of the radical "anti-mainstream" faction of the JTU. The Nichū teacher who was elected vice-chairman of the youth division, in the second slate of nominees, explained, "The anti-mainstream factions of the JTU were in control of the Nippon City youth section. There were all kinds of communist-style movements and opposition to educational officials. This year we decided to stand up. Up to now, five or six members dominated 120 members of the youth division. But we are not a principals' union. We are not going to be used by the principals. But then we are not a real labor union, either."

As it happened, the slate of nominees, first proposed during the meeting had been drawn up by the youth division officers. Rather than enter a second slate of candidates in direct opposition to the first slate, the moderate dissenters had decided to vote against the officers' slate and then put up their own candidates for election.

The second slate of candidates had, in fact, been chosen far in advance of the meeting, with the candidates informally agreeing to serve, if elected. Communication among the teachers had been sufficiently good to let them know that a second slate was available so that they would vote against the first slate. This activity had apparently gone on without the knowledge of the former youth division leaders so that they were truly surprised to find themselves out of power after the election.

One of the moderate candidates had actually been selected for inclusion in the first slate of nominees, but had withdrawn his name several weeks before the general meeting when he was told of the formation of a second slate of nominees. He was then elected in the second slate.

Two of the four nominees in the first slate were the two Tokai teachers who had been transferred the preceding year without their consent and had caused the *shibu* meeting that year the troubles described previously.

The underlying structure of such meetings in Japanese society is obviously well-organized. The outward form of a nominating committee, chosen ostensibly on the spur of the moment, conceals the fact that candidates have been effectively elected by a different procedure earlier. Another example of this procedure has already been given in the description of the Nichū PTA election of officers.

That the union organization also fulfills a social function was evident in the sponsorship of an annual *bōnenkai* (year-end party) for youth section members on Christmas day at a local restaurant. Strictly an occasion for drinking *sake* and renewing friendships, the young teachers looked forward to the occasion.

During the winter vacation, one of the Nichū teachers mentioned above participated in a two-day "labor course" sponsored by the youth section of the prefectural teachers union. According to his description the meeting included people who are very extreme in union affairs. He said that the youth section of the prefectural union had the same problems of leadership as the Nippon City youth section. The prefectural union had not, however, ousted the radical leadership.

Much emphasis is placed on research and study for teachers in both their union and nonunion activities. A large annual educational research meeting is sponsored on a nationwide basis by the JTU as the culmination of research activities at the prefectural and local levels. Most prefectures, too, have a teachers' union-sponsored annual meeting for reports of educational research conducted within the prefecture during the previous year.

At the local level, the teachers' union *shibu* organized "research circles" to bring together teachers interested in study and research related to specific topics. At Nichū school, the *shibu* executive committee representative made an announcement in July about the planning meeting for local research circles which would be held the following week. Each school was to send several representatives to the central meeting for the *shibu* which would discuss topics to be prepared for the annual prefectural educational research meeting in November.

One of the Nichū representatives to the *shibu* general committee went to represent the Nichū teachers. There were no *shidō shuji,* or school principals, in attendance at the meeting. Discussion centered on the preparation of research reports that would be taken to both the prefectural and national educational research meetings.

According to the general schedule for research activities outlined on the program for the planning meeting, the months of April to August were to be used for research activity and writing of reports at the local schools. September and October were to be used for research circle activities and discussion of the individual reports. The prefectural research meeting was scheduled for the second week in November, on a Saturday and Sunday, to give many teachers the opportunity to attend.

In spite of the lack of organization or enthusiasm at the Nippon City planning meeting, the prefectural educational research meeting did not reflect this spirit. Although the organization of the prefectural meeting was atypical for Japan, it represented a most interesting pattern of cooperation between union and administrative educational groups.

The meetings attended by the author, many of the Nichū teachers, and more than a thousand of the prefecture's elementary and middle school teachers were held on the campus of the prefectural university's school of education. It was called the "Seventh Annual Educational Research Assembly" of the "Prefectural Educational Research Federation." Official sponsorship of the meeting was not listed on the printed program though one assumed that it was to be the prefectural level meeting in preparation for the national research meeting sponsored publicly by the JTU.

In the early postwar years, two prefectural-level educational research meetings had been held annually. One was sponsored by the prefectural university's school of education and was a continuation of similar prewar meetings organized by the prefectural normal school which was the predecessor of the school of education. The second annual meeting had been sponsored by the prefectural teachers union. At the request of the teachers, a combined educational research meeting was organized through the cooperation of the union and the school of education to eliminate the duplication of educational research reports that had been occurring. Because the prefectural education office had cooperated earlier in the university-sponsored research meetings, they continued to cooperate with the new prefectural research organization in spite of the union affiliation. This cooperation consisted mainly of inclusion of the prefectural education office's guidance section staff of *shidō shuji* in the program as advisers for each of the separate research sections. Thus official sponsorship of the meetings rested with the university and the union, but the education office was included in the planning and conduct of the meetings.

In the year of this study, the Ministry of Education had announced a new plan for a nationwide research organization, covertly designed to compete with the JTU's nationwide organization of educational research by classroom teachers. The new plan did not call for prefectural research meetings, however, and so did not interfere with the conduct of the university and union-sponsored meeting in the prefecture of this study.

Thus professional research activities were an important element of teachers union activities at all levels, though particularly at the prefectural and national level of organization. In general, they complemented, rather than conflicted with, the study and research activities organized by the administrative community at the local level. In this area of union activity, the union was cast much more in the pattern of a professional educators' association than a labor union.

UNION ACTIVITY WITHIN NICHŪ

Union-related activities observed in Nichū school by the author were mainly extensions of activities initiated at higher levels of the union. Only one formal teachers union *bunkai* meeting was observed, though more may have been held. The major intrusion of union matters into the school occurred when announcements were made about union business during the regular teachers' meeting before or after school in the teachers' room.

Early in the school year, three teachers were elected to teachers union *bunkai* positions. The election took place during a Nichū teachers' meeting. The three teachers elected were to represent the *bunkai* on the *shibu* committees, two on the general committee and one on the executive committee.

Six days before the national achievement tests were scheduled to be administered, a formal Nichū *bunkai* meeting was called in the afternoon after classes. Though the meeting was not listed among the week's activities on the head teacher's blackboard, the word had been passed to the teachers. The representative to the *shibu* executive committee chaired the meeting which was held in the teachers' room in a fashion similar to all Nichū teachers' meetings. He moved from his own desk to the principal's desk at the head of the room to call the meeting to order. Later the principal came in and pulled a chair to one side of the desk for himself.

The first item of business was a report from one of the Nichū teachers who served as representative on the *shibu* general committee. He presented a list of five problems that had been discussed at a meeting of his committee, one of which was the problem of the nationwide achievement tests. The conference of the *shibu* representatives with the Nippon City superintendent of education was mentioned in this report. Then the Nichū teachers were asked to express their opinions.

Much in the manner of everyday Nichū teachers' meetings, the teachers were sitting at their desks, correcting students' homework or carrying out other small chores, without giving the impression that they were paying much attention to the discussion at hand. A few teachers, however, did express their opinions. One older teacher expressed a strong concern for the way in which the test results would be used. Another teacher, answering his arguments, said, "When you get to be a principal, your opinion will change." Most of the teachers laughed at this, but it did start a tangential discussion of the role of the principal and head teacher. An older teacher, classmate of the principal, turned to both the principal and head teacher and said, "It really must be difficult for you."

Going back to the discussion about the achievement tests, the chairman asked what conclusions should be drawn from the *bunkai* discussion. The *shibu* general committee representative replied, "After all, we are all employees, so we cannot do much but submit a petition."

At the end of the meeting, a petition opposing the achievement tests was passed around for the teachers' signatures by the chairman.

Less than an hour and a half after the opening of the meeting, the chairman brought it to a close. The major accomplishment was the signing of the anti-achievement test petition.

After the achievement tests had been carried out with the full cooperation of the Nichū teachers, the *shibu* executive committee representative reported at a teachers' meeting that the committee was collecting criticisms of the test and would like each *bunkai* to hold a special meeting to make their criticisms. Because Nichū teachers had a very busy schedule, however, he suggested that the teachers speak to him individually about their criticisms and he would then relay them to the committee.

Several months later on their way to attend the prefectural educational research meeting, the executive committee representative and several other teachers from different Nippon City schools were discussing union activities with the author. An example that was given of the lack of activity in the Nippon City teachers union *shibu* referred to the call for local school meetings in opposition to the achievement tests. According to the teachers, the JTU central office had called the meetings and specified that they all be held at 9 A.M. on a given day. The prefectural teachers union office thought this was an inconvenient time and so suggested that the meetings be held at 1 P.M. in the prefecture of Nippon City. The Nippon City *shibu,* however, thought this timing inconvenient too, and suggested meetings at 3 P.M. By the time the call for the meetings had reached the individual schools, there was a great deal of variation—and Nichū had not even held a formal meeting.

During the period of this study, a national election for members of the Diet's House of Councillors was held. The House of Councillors has 250 members of whom 150 are elected from the prefectures and 100 are elected from the nation at large. Each voter is allowed to vote for one prefectural candidate and one national candidate. One of the candidates running at large in the election was the JTU national chairman, Takeshi Kobayashi. Though officially a candidate of the Socialist party, he based his successful campaign on his teachers union affiliation, and used teachers union channels of communication to promote his election.

About a month before the election, the Nichū *shibu* executive committee representative announced at an early morning teachers' meeting that the campaign for Kobayashi's election had been discussed by the committee. He passed out to the teachers several campaign leaflets which were imprinted with the name of an organization called the "Japanese Federation of Democratic Education and Government." Though the name of the JTU did not appear, Kobayashi's positions with the union were given in the biographical data on the leaflets.

Also passed out were some postcards endorsing Kobayashi's candidacy. The teachers were asked to address the postcards to a friend and to sign their names. They were then collected by the executive committee representative to arrange for postage and mailing. All the teachers appeared to sign the cards.

In November the executive committee representative introduced a new teachers union project to the teachers at the regular before-school teachers' meeting. This time, the union was interested in a survey which would show the number of hours actually worked by teachers over and above the regular working day. Forms were passed out to each teacher on which they could record overtime work performed at school in cne column and homework in a second column. The starting date of the survey was clearly specified, though no ending date appeared to be set. The form allowed space for three weeks of reporting.

The representative explained that the purpose of the survey was to show that there was a shortage of teachers and that the present pay was insufficient. "After all, in a usual company the people only work until 4:30 and then they are through," he said.

The above examples are representative of the conduct of union business within the school. The teachers and principal never objected to the conduct of such business during school hours or teaching meetings. Union activities had a professional aura and were considered appropriate for discussion and concern in regular school gatherings.

INFORMAL TEACHER ACTIVITIES

Not all the organized activities for Nichū teachers were strictly professional. Similar in pattern to the organized recreational activities of other employed groups, particularly in white-collar occupations, there were plans for group recreational activities which would include all of the teachers. At the end of each of the three school terms during the year, it was general practice to organize a "meeting for reflection." When first invited to such a meeting, the author assumed that it would include some form of professional evaluation of the school term just completed. His suspicions were aroused, however, by the location of the meeting at one of the restaurants near the center of Nippon City.

The occasion turned out to be a full-scale party with beer and food for all. Local Nichū District merchants and the PTA chairman donated some of the food and drink which was appropriately acknowledged by the principal at the start of the party. There were no formalities beyond the first toast led by the principal. As time wore on, the men's shirts came off and they began to sing. The female teachers and school lunch cook retreated to one end of the room and talked together. At different times, two of the younger male teachers were asleep on the floor. When one of the younger male teachers began an argument with an older teacher that could not be amicably settled, the party came to a close "because the next party was waiting to get into the room." The argument was not treated seriously, rather, it was the signal that the party had gone on long enough. Each teacher warned the others to be careful on their way home, and they left the restaurant.

At a second such party, the higher PTA officers were invited to join with the teachers in their celebration of the end of the second term. The officials came and were included as full members of the group. The party at the end of the year, after the graduation ceremony, was sponsored by the PTA and the teachers were invited guests.

During the summer vacation, a good deal of planning and anticipation went into a trip by the Nichū teachers to a local resort. Spending only one night and two days there, it was noteworthy to the American researcher that wives and husbands were not included in such an affair. Since the teachers worked together as a group, they were the ones who went together on their vacation trip.

Having now completed our description of the Nichū school and its relations with the local and national society, the following chapter takes us back once again to the school and especially to the people who direct the process of education, the classroom teachers. Where they come from, the way in which they view their professional responsibilities, and the variation which they demonstrate under exposure to the cross-fire of local and national forces, helps us to understand the process and effects of school education which they direct in their Nichū classrooms.

8 / The Nichū teachers

NICHŪ SCHOOL TEACHERS were primarily long-time residents of the prefecture in which the school is located, some with prewar teaching experience and some without it. There is, in Japan, little job mobility from one employer to another or from one occupation to another. Having started as teachers, they looked forward to remaining teachers for the rest of their working lives, subject to the assignments made by their employer, the prefectural Board of Education. Some had planned from childhood to be teachers, while others had drifted into teaching jobs at the end of their higher education or had used teaching positions as an escape from unpleasant situations. But, once started, none contemplated change.

As individuals, their life histories were diverse and relevant to their present positions and attitudes. They came from, and lived in, a variety of different circumstances, though only one recalled his childhood home being poorer economically than the average of his neighborhood. Respectable, average members of society from both rural and urban homes, they continued to perform a variety of individual social roles in addition to the common one of teacher.

Five of the Nichū teachers were women, four of whom were married. Three of the women were married to teachers in other schools, while six of the eighteen married male teachers had wives teaching in the public schools. All the married female teachers had children, but they left their teaching responsibilities only for the period of maternity leave.

The proportion of older teachers was slightly higher than usual because the desirable location of the school meant that older teachers could exercise their rights of seniority to arrange transfers to Nichū. One man had left a higher-prestige job as head teacher of an elementary school, a job he had held for ten years, to come to Nichū as a classroom teacher, because he wanted to live in Nippon City.

All but one of the Nichū teachers was born in the local prefecture. The lone exception was the son of local parents who emigrated to Korea, returning to their previous home at the end of World War II. Only one teacher went outside of the prefecture for his secondary education, though nine had left the prefecture for higher education. Eight teachers were graduates of high schools or prewar *chūgakkō* located in Nippon City.

Eight of the teachers considered themselves permanent residents of Nippon City since it was their official address of record (*honseki*) for government matters.

Three of them had official addresses within the Nichū District. Three more teachers actually resided within the school district but maintained their permanent addresses elsewhere. Thus a significant proportion of the teachers were permanently connected with the local community.

The author's initial assumption was that most teachers would turn out to be the younger sons from local families who established themselves in a new profession outside the family, while the eldest son carried on the family profession, business, or farm. But this was not upheld at Nichū or other schools visited. Nine of the Nichū male teachers were eldest sons of their families and four of these were from farm homes, where they might have been expected to carry on the family farm as a full time occupation.

Six more of the married male teachers were adopted husbands who took their wives' family names at marriage and were responsible for the continuity of their wives' families. In this fashion, they carried the responsibility of eldest sons in their adoptive families. Teachers are considered especially desirable as adoptive husbands by families who are searching for men to marry their daughters and continue their family lines. Because of the teacher's role in the community, he is not expected to be tempted by the vices that lead ordinary husbands astray. There is a better chance that he will be a model husband for the daughter.

In all, seventeen of the twenty-two married teachers, male and female, were in a direct line of family succession responsible for the continuation of their family line.

Two of the male teachers lived on family farms within the Nippon City limits and continued their farming with the "weekend and womenfolk" pattern. Neither participated as much as other teachers in extracurricular activities of the school. The one unmarried female teacher, a twenty-two-year-old girl, continued to live with her parents on their farm near Nippon City. A third, male teacher also lived on a family farm but, because he had been under treatment for tuberculosis for many years, had to leave all the work to his wife and her parents. As an adopted husband, he had responsibility for carrying on the family line, but he was not able to carry the responsibility for the farm.

Though the pattern of "weekend and womenfolk" farming is a common one in Japan, it is not maintained without some strain. The author and his wife attended a meeting of the women's group in the isolated farm *buraku* where one of the Nichū teacher-farmers lived. Throughout the social get-together, which included a meal, the teacher, who had escorted them to the meeting, was teased about the manner in which he made his wife do the heavy work on the farm while he had an "easy" white-collar job. The other women made very pointed remarks about the fact that his wife had to eat several more bowls of rice at a meal than he to maintain her energy for her heavy farm labor.

He later described the conflict with his elderly parents, who were unable to accept the idea that teaching was anything but a supplementary occupation. To them, the work of the family farm always came first and he had to pacify them by working very diligently on the farm in his spare time.

Six of the teachers came from families in which their fathers had been teachers.

The head teacher's father had left a farm home, though he was the eldest son, to become a teacher. The head teacher, his four sisters, and his wife were all teachers. Evidently, in this case, the family profession was teaching.

One female English teacher was the only child of two teacher-parents. To assure continuity in the family line, a husband was adopted into the family for her. The man chosen for this honor was an English teacher and the two planned to continue their teaching. During the first part of this study, she was on maternity leave with her first child. When her leave expired, she left the baby in the care of her retired mother while she returned to work.

Originally, eleven of the teachers came from farm homes. Five of these were eldest sons, though there was only one, mentioned above, who kept the family farm going.

Of the seventeen teachers who received their professional education before or during the war, eight had attended the prefectural normal school, six had attended a variety of specialized schools in Tokyo, one had taken a six-month short course for teachers given in Nippon City about 1930, one had attended the normal school in Sakhalin, and one had not received any special professional education beyond graduation from the top academic prewar middle school in the prefecture.

Among those who received their professional education after the end of the war, there were three who had attended the School of Education of the local prefectural university, one who had been a student of the prefectural College of Agriculture, and three who had attended institutions of higher education in Tokyo. One teacher in the latter group was a graduate of Waseda University, one of the best private universities in Japan.

Ten teachers actually began their teaching in the prewar or wartime period. Nine were elementary school teachers then, though some had responsibility for the *kōtō shōgakkō* (higher elementary school) classes in their schools. The other one had been a teacher in a private middle school operated and owned by her father.

Five of the fourteen teachers who began their teaching careers after the war also started as elementary school teachers, later transferring to middle school positions.

As automobiles are often symbolic of the owners' socio-economic status in America, vehicular transportation in Japan, too, can give an indication of class position. About half of the teachers owned motorscooters or light motorcycles, the Japanese middle-class vehicle. Though some urban and upper-class families owned autos in Nippon City, the first farm home to acquire an automobile in Uena Region did so during the period of this study. Other teachers rode bicycles or commuted to work by bus or train.

Seven of the teachers had joined together to form an automobile club. Putting in equal amounts of money, they purchased a second-hand taxi which they used during school hours for business and after school hours on a rotating basis for recreational trips. Four of the five Nippon City middle school faculties owned automobiles in this way and were quite proud of their prestigious transportation. Many of the teachers, even those not included in the "club," were taking automobile driving lessons in local driving schools, a recent innovation in the Japanese countryside.

BETWEEN THE UNION AND THE MINISTRY

One of the major goals of the field study was to understand the individual teacher's sense of identification with the different groups that impinge upon the school; to see the ways in which the teachers perceive and resolve the conflicting pressures and national positions of the Ministry of Education and the Japan Teachers Union.

Data from interviews with the teachers suggest that the teachers feel a sense of isolation from both those national organizations, but, also, a sense of loyalty to both. Within this conscious framework, they are able to make their own decisions about individual positions on educational issues. Publicly, however, they must support the JTU's struggles *and* the Ministry of Education's directives. They try to do both, even when there is a logical conflict. Privately, they reserve the right to their own opinions which are often directly contradictory to their public stands. That their expressed opinions and private actions are often contradictory is indicative of the pressures upon them.

The single most pervasive opinion expressed by the teachers in private interviews with the author was the idea that it is very important to have a powerful, national teachers union which will be able to counter the extension of the Ministry of Education's power in the control of public education. Eleven of the older teachers and ten of the younger ones expressed this idea directly or implied it strongly in their discussion of the two organizations.

Only one teacher expressed complete opposition to the JTU without the qualifying implication given by the others that it was necessary as an organization to counter the Ministry of Education's influence. Yet, this teacher did not express any desire to quit the union.

One older male teacher, with ten years of prewar teaching experience said, "The union is necessary. If it were not for the union, the Ministry of Education would gradually get stronger and stronger. When compared with the past, it would not be good for this to happen." Another older male teacher said, "There is a feeling that if the Ministry of Education gets too strong, education will be warped."

After criticizing the JTU for its separation from the teachers and saying that he would like to quit the union, if he could, an older teacher added, "But if there was no union, we would be in a bad way, too." Other older male teachers said in a similar manner:

> We teachers do not want to enter political struggles, but they have to be carried on to protect our livelihood. Therefore, the JTU is a necessary institution.

> The conflict between JTU and the Ministry of Education is necessary for the sake of the teachers' livelihood and for the sake of the demands of the society at large. These kinds of demands are gradually being taken up by the JTU. . . . Among the demands of the society at large being taken up by the JTU are the movement to admit all children to high school, the idea that all educational expenses should be paid by the nation, etc. Up to now, Socialist party and Communist party demands have been many; up to now the teachers union has been separated from the teacher, but this is changing now.

I do not like the JTU or the union very much. If the JTU was not there, however, the Ministry of Education could order anything it wanted, so it is good to have the JTU there.

A younger teacher expressed himself in much the same way: "The conflict is necessary. It cannot be said that the Ministry of Education's educational views are all correct. It is the JTU's job to interject the voice of the teachers who are working in the schools. There is a need for discussion between the JTU and the Ministry of Education. It is too bad, though, that relations between the two organizations are so bad."

Along with this feeling that it is necessary to have a union which will counterbalance and restrain the Ministry of Education is a sense of responsibility to the union. Teachers feel that being teachers, they must join the union. Then, as members of the union, they must support its struggles against the Ministry of Education, regardless of their personal opinions about a given issue. Solidarity is an important goal of both trade unions and professional organizations in any country. To achieve solidarity, both ideological and social pressures are generated. Among Nichū teachers, the pressures for union membership have been irresistable.

One older teacher described his desire to get out of the union: "I really wanted to escape from the union, but I have not been able to do it. . . . In Nippon City, of 300 teachers, none have left the JTU. Oh, yes, I have heard that one elementary school teacher left . . . he refuses to pay his dues. To leave, one has to have courage. If one of twenty-some teachers leaves, he has to be ready to forego friendly intercourse with others. If one leaves the union, he gives the feeling of being non-cooperative, non-harmonious. I do not want to be thought of like that."

There was an underlying assumption that one cannot leave the union, though there is no legal restriction upon the teacher to join. For instance, one older teacher said, "If I could, I would like to quit the JTU."

A specific instance of union solidarity occurred when most of the teachers signed the union-sponsored petition against the giving of annual national achievement examinations by the Ministry of Education. In privately-expressed positions, ten of the older and nine of the younger teachers expressed no concern about the Ministry of Education giving such examinations. When asked about the petition, they indicated that they had signed as an indication of support for the union, rather than as an indication of their personal opinion.

An older male teacher said, "I signed the petition for the sake of the union, but it was not my real opinion."

A younger teacher who approved of the national achievement examinations said, "I signed the petition as a member of the union." He did not feel it necessary to explain any inconsistency.

Another said, "Since everybody signed the petition against the achievement tests, I did, too. Regardless of our opinions, we are all members of the union and we all signed. But that was inconsistent."

Three older and two younger teachers did agree with the JTU's position. A younger teacher said she signed the petition as an expression of her own opinion. "I signed the petition opposing the achievement tests and I really oppose them.

The Ministry of Education is not thinking at all about the local control of education."

A second general opinion of the JTU, expressed by seven of the older teachers and three of the younger ones was that it does not really represent the views of Japanese teachers, especially in its political conflicts with the Government.

One older male teacher said, in explanation of the conflict between the Ministry of Education and the JTU: "The fundamental reason of conflict is really the fact that the JTU does not represent the general will of the Japanese teachers. We, as members, do not consider the political relations of the union; they are decided by the Union's main office. Generally the teachers think differently than the Union. The JTU is not really representative of the Japanese teachers. The teachers are not really unified behind the JTU struggles."

Another member of the older teachers' group felt that the gap between the union and its members' way of thinking was getting wider. "The opinion of the general union members, as far as the JTU is concerned, has been changing. The union spirit is becoming very weak. However, the spirit of the national JTU officers is strong. Therefore, the thinking of the national office and the general membership is drifting apart."

Referring to the JTU's struggle against the merit rating system introduced on a compulsory basis by the Ministry of Education, an older teacher said, "We weren't really worried about the problem, but we had to carry out the union's struggle."

In the political realm, an older teacher said, "The leaders of the JTU are Socialists, but the teachers, in general, are not clearly identified with this idea. The teachers generally know the bad points of socialism and communism."

Expressing his sense of alienation from JTU policy formulation, an older teacher said, "Of course we all enter the JTU, but JTU opinions are formed by only one group, the officials. Policy is formed at the top, not at the bottom."

Two teachers used the word "radical" in describing the JTU. One younger teacher said, "The JTU has been too radical. It needs to think more about the feelings of the classroom teachers. My feeling is that there is a real separation between the JTU and the teachers. The reason for this is that problems like peace and atom bomb testing have taken up too much of JTU activities. There has not been enough attention paid to educational problems."

Of particular interest, for an analysis of the teachers' relationship to the JTU and the Ministry of Education, were the teachers' responses to questions that touched on five current major issues of contention at the national level. They were asked to express their opinions on the issues directly, without reference by the interviewer to any connection with JTU—Ministry of Education controversy. The answers were then coded to show agreement or disagreement with the Ministry of Education's position and any suspicion of the Ministry's intentions in proposing or enforcing the actions concerned.

The answers to these questions are summarized in Table 10.

Most surprising, for those who consider the JTU to be the spokesman for Japanese teachers, is the large amount of agreement expressed with the Ministry's proposals and actions by both the younger and older teachers. Though all five issues had aroused intense opposition by the national JTU, and demonstrations had been

TABLE 10

NICHŪ TEACHERS' POSITIONS ON CONTEMPORARY EDUCATIONAL ISSUES

Issue	Older Teachers (N = 13)			Younger Teachers (N = 11)		
	Agree	Disagree	Suspicious of Ministry's Intentions	Agree	Disagree	Suspicious of Ministry's Intentions
1. Promulgation of new middle school curriculum by the Ministry of Education. (Disagree means some criticism of curriculum expressed.)	9	1	–	5	4	–
2. National achievement test given by Ministry of Education in all middle schools.	10	3	2	9	2	4
3. Merit rating system for teachers required by Ministry and performed by school principals.	6	6	–	1	7	2
4. Ministry of Education proposal for a national curriculum in teacher education and a national certification system.	5	1	3	5	3	2
5. Minister of Education's proposal for a national textbook to be prepared for *dōtoku* classes.	8	3	2	5	6	2
Total teachers expressing any suspicions of Ministry intentions with respect to these issues.			6			6

carried out throughout the country expressing opposition to the Ministry's position on the first three issues, only the merit rating system was opposed by a majority of the Nichū teachers.

Though twenty-one teachers expressed their support of the union as a counterbalance to the Ministry of Education, as mentioned above, only six of the older and six of the younger teachers expressed or implied any suspicion of the Ministry of Education's position on the five issues. Several, of course, expressed their suspicions on more than one of the issues. The suspicions were related to views of the Ministry of Education's actions as intended to lead toward more centralized control of education.

An older teacher, giving his opinion of the national achievement tests, said, "If the Ministry of Education follows the purposes it said, then the tests would be good. But this is probably not the case."

Two younger teachers made their suspicions more explicit: "The Ministry of Education may use these tests as material for the appraisal of teachers, and that is bad." "The Ministry of Education seems to be trying to measure compliance with the new curriculum rather than the students' real achievement. Just like the JTU, I'm against the tests."

Criticism of the merit rating system introduced by the Ministry of Education was most widespread among the Nichū teachers. This seemed to be motivated more by personal, defensive reactions or criticism of the system employed, than by fear of the Ministry of Education's intentions. Only two younger teachers indicated any such suspicions. "The system is for the purpose of enforcing Ministry of Education orders. A bad teacher is one who does not do what the Ministry says."

Two younger and two older teachers saw the proposal for a national morals education textbook as an attempt by the Ministry to gain more control over a part of the school's curriculum. One older teacher said, "It might become like the old *shūshin,* which is probably the idea of the Minister of Education."

Though one older teacher and four younger ones expressed some criticism of the new Ministry of Education curriculum for middle schools, none did so on the basis that the Ministry was trying to exert too much control over the schools. This is noteworthy because of the large amount of publicity given to the JTU's opposition to the curriculum for that reason.

In describing their reactions to conflict between the Ministry of Education and the JTU, five of the older teachers and one of the younger ones referred to the political connections of the JTU with the Socialist party. Two of the older teachers and the younger one also referred to the Ministry of Education's position as a representative of the Liberal-Democratic Party-controlled Government. If they had been asked directly about political affiliations of these organizations, of course, most of the teachers would have identified them in the same way. The important point is that so few teachers thought to identify the political party affiliations of the JTU and the Ministry in explaining their own reaction to the conflict between them.

Slipped into the beginning of each teacher interview, along with information on personal history, was a question about political party preference and the person's vote in the last Diet election, held during the period of this study. The second question was asked specifically to see how many teachers had voted for the JTU candidate in the election, formerly the head official of the national union, who ran as a Socialist with intensive support from the JTU. Fourteen of the twenty-four teachers said that they had voted for the JTU candidate. Whether or not they actually had voted this way, their answers to the interviewer indicated their loyalty, in practice, to the JTU.

Two of the younger teachers expressed conflicting points of view that reflected concerns of many Japanese teachers for the future course of the JTU. One expressed the view that the JTU is a labor union, the official view of the national JTU. The other expressed a hope that it would become more of a professional teachers' association.

The first one said, "Since we are laborers, we need a union to protect our livelihood. This is necessary, even in the struggles. In order to raise our standard of living, that kind of struggle is necessary." The second teacher stated, "As a union of teachers, there are occasions where the JTU has gone too far. It should be different from other unions. It should be more like a teachers union . . . The JTU has cooperated with other unions in many activities, but I think it would be better for it to stick strictly to activities related to teachers."

Though the idea of the JTU as a labor union is a controversial one in Japanese educational circles, eight of the older Nichū teachers and six of the younger ones approved this view explicitly, or implied their acceptance of it, when they expressed their support of the union for its activity in improving the teachers' livelihood. Three teachers specifically mentioned the fact that adequate maternity leave privileges had been won for female teachers by the activity of the union.

One older female teacher pointed to one of the Nichū teachers who had just come back to work from six months of maternity leave and said: "She was able to have a leisurely maternity leave. This is because of the union influence. In my day, we had to work up until the day our child was born."

An older male teacher recounted for the author the story of an early teachers' movement in which his father had been a leader for better teachers' salaries. During World War I, the teachers in one of the regions of the prefecture had organized to demand higher wages from the prefectural governor. There was an argument, and the Minister of Education became involved. The teachers who led the movement, however, were all reassigned to different and distant schools as punishment for their activity. It would seem, therefore, that the idea of a teachers' union interested in advancing the teachers' working conditions is not strictly a postwar phenomena (cf. Kitamura 1962: 76–80).

It can be seen that both the younger and the older teachers support the JTU for two major reasons: (1) for offsetting the power that the Ministry of Education might develop in its control of public education and (2) for the improvement which it can bring in teachers' working conditions and livelihood. The teachers feel a necessity to support the union's activities, whether or not they are in personal agreement with the specific issues involved. But they do not accept the JTU's or the Ministry's leadership on professional issues without question. They are placed in, and maintain, an ambivalent position with respect to the conflict between the JTU and the Ministry.

Discussing the conflict at the national level, one of the older female teachers said, "There has been too much conflict, too much difference of opinions. I would like to see them both come a little closer together. It is good that there are two organizations, though. If there were only one, there would be only one line of thought. But the differences are too great. I do not like to choose sides between the JTU and the Ministry, but the Ministry is too strong. In spite of the JTU opposition, the national achievement tests were carried out."

The most extreme example of internal conflict and ambivalence among the Nichū teachers was the older man they had elected to be representative on the executive committee of the Nippon City Teachers Union. He had acquired extensive teaching experience before the war and had opposed the formation of the JTU in the postwar period. He was opposed to the union formation on what he called "Buddhist philosophical principles." One should not push for himself, but be contented with what he is granted by others. As a teacher, he did not feel that he should fight for better living conditions for teachers at the expense of other groups.

Though he had joined the union, he never felt attracted to its major purposes as a labor union or as an anti-Ministry educational organization. He had accepted the responsibility of being Nichū's union representative with a great deal of reluctance and trepidation.

"When I told one of the other teachers I wanted to get out of the job, he said I should stay in and apply the brakes instead."

As the local union representative, he had the responsibility for communicating union information to the teachers. This he did with outward equanimity, though he was personally opposed to most of the activities which he was supposed to be leading for the union among the Nichū teachers. Thus he distributed campaign literature to the teachers on behalf of the JTU candidate for the Diet and organized a postcard mailing from the Nichū teachers to their friends on the candidate's behalf; but he, himself, did not vote in that election. He identified himself with the Liberal-Democratic party. At another time he brought the anti-achievement test petition to Nichū and passed it around for the teachers' signatures, explaining the basis of the union's concern in this affair. He did not indicate to the teachers his own personal opposition to this struggle, and claims that he did not sign the petition himself. He told the author that all the teachers except the principal and head teacher had signed the petition, though several teachers later denied to the author that they had signed it.

The interesting, and perhaps representative, feature of this man's relationship to the JTU was the way in which he personally rejected the basic principles of the union; yet, when called upon to perform an active role in the furtherance of union concerns, he energetically fulfilled the distasteful personal responsibilities that had been thrust upon him by his fellow teachers.

In somewhat exaggerated form, this man represented the conflicts felt by a majority of the teachers. He also represented the resolution of these conflicts through the fulfillment of his obligations to his fellow teachers in service to the union. He was able to separate his personal feelings from his roles as a Nichū teacher and union member, but he could not shirk his responsibility to his fellow Nichū teachers. Nichū teacher unity was an important value to him.

TEACHERS' ROLE BEHAVIOR

Nichū teachers are not easily described as a group. They vary significantly as individuals in a variety of different ways. Five dimensions of teacher role behavior can be suggested, however, through the translation of five Japanese terms. Each can be described as a specific definition of appropriate teacher role behavior, one not necessarily consistent with the others. While individual teachers cannot be placed neatly by these words into categories, their specific behaviors, attitudes, and perceptions can be so classified.

If the appropriate teacher behavior was to be accurately measured, a profile could be drawn for an individual teacher describing the proportional influence of these role definitions on his perception of himself, on the observed activity of teachres in the school environment, on parents' expectations or perceptions of teacher behavior, or in other ways of describing relevant role expectations and performance.

The roles are best described by five Japanese terms, the connotations of which can be rendered into English, though precise translation is impossible. Using the common English translations of the Japanese terms would be confusing because of the different connotations of the English translations.

The five Japanese terms are *sensei, kyōin, rōdōsha, kenkyūsha* and *gakusha.* Both *sensei* and *kyōin* are usually translated as "teacher"; *rōdōsha* as "laborer"; *kenkyūsha* as "researcher"; and *gakusha* as "scholar."

Sensei is the word used most in talking about individual teachers. It is a respectful term and is used in place of the suffix *-san* (Mr., Mrs., Miss) with the names of teachers, doctors, professors, priests, or people who are especially deserving of respect. Teachers of traditional arts or sports are always referred to as *sensei*. The author was usually called Singleton-*sensei* by the people of Nippon City who viewed him as associated with the school. Nichū teachers, however, called him Singleton-*san,* because he had no official position within the school. *Sensei* is also used by teachers as a first or second person pronoun when talking with each other or with their pupils, as mentioned earlier. When used as a noun, the honorific connotations are still implied.

By way of contrast, *kyōin* refers specifically to school teachers, instructors, or educators. It is never used with personal names in the way that *sensei* is used. The Japanese characters used to write *kyōin* can be translated "employee of an educational institution." The overtones of *kyōin* carry the idea of a white-collar employee or a *sarariman,* which is the Japanese language transcription of "salary man." It is the *sarariman* who has a regular salaried middle class job, lives in the suburbs, and represents the modern Japanese family ideal.

The word *sensei,* on the other hand, connotes a dedicated teacher in the traditional fashion, who is reluctant to accept compensation for his services, but to whom a pupil incurs an unending obligation (*on*). It carries no *sarariman* connotation (compare Benedict 1946: 103).

A *rōdōsha* is literally one who labors. *Rōdō* means "to labor" and is used in the phrase *rōdō kumiai* to mean a modern labor union. It is associated with the Marxist analysis of society and an explicit emphasis on the laboring class. The word is important to teachers because the JTU lays great stress on the identification of teachers as *rōdōsha*, justifying itself as a trade union and its participation with other trade unions in *Sohyo*, the General Council of Japanese Trade Unions. The word *rōdōsha* then implies a different connotation from the *sarariman* emphasis of *kyōin*, with a specific political emphasis identifying the *rōdōsha* with the Marxist-defined working class.

A scholar or learned man is known as a *gakusha*. This is a term implying traditional respect and status. It has moral overtones implying a man who would be a model of good behavior because of his erudition. On the other hand, *kenkyūsha* refers to a researcher. The verb *kenkyū* means "to study" as well as "to do research" and is much used in educational circles. *Kenkyūsha* is literally "one who studies" and implies involvement in a process rather than referring to a great store of learning, the connotation of *gakusha*. Almost all meetings of teachers are called *kenkyūkai* or "study meetings" regardless of their purpose. Both the JTU and the Ministry of Education stress the importance of *kenkyū* activities for teachers and this idea is very much a part of the modern professional image of teachers.

The words *gakusha* and *sensei* are related and carry similar implications. They would be used in describing the traditional ideal teacher. *Kyōin* and *kenkyūsha* are similarly related and would be used in describing a newer concept of the teacher.

The ideal teacher from a JTU point of view would combine *kyōin, kenkyūsha,* and *rōdōsha* attributes. The JTU is a *kyōin kumiai* (teachers' union) and stresses in its official "Teacher's Code of Ethics" that "teachers are engaged in the establishment of scientific truth" and that "teachers are *rōdōsha.*" These statements are directly related to the *kenkyūsha* and *rōdōsha* role dimensions, respectively.

Specific distinctions between the teacher role definitions implied by these five terms, which the author believes can be made, are given in Table 11. Blank spaces in the table indicate areas where there is no specific teacher role implication. It can be seen that the *sensei* and *kyōin* role definitions carry the most implications for teacher behavior. The *rōdōsha, kenkyūsha,* and *gakusha* roles are supplementary.

A teacher whose actions and perceptions of self were both high in the *sensei* dimension of teacher role behavior was Mr. Tanaka, the strict and severe morals education specialist of Nichū. One of the older teachers group, he had been born as the second son in a farm home within the Nichū District. As a young man, he went off to Sakhalin. There he entered normal school and became a teacher of the higher elementary schools. In 1947 he was repatriated to Nippon City and began teaching at a nearby elementary school until the new middle school was formed. He then transferred to Nichū and at the time of the study was the teacher with the longest term of service at Nichū. He enrolled in extension courses of Keio University and received his bachelor's degree after four years of study in 1955, though he had not left his teaching job.

With many of his students, particularly the academically able, he developed a very close relationship. This was evident in observations of the author when Mr. Tanaka talked with students and their parents during home visits and when former students came back to Nichū specifically to see him. It was he, during the teacher

TABLE 11

IMPLICATIONS OF FIVE ROLE DEFINITIONS AMONG JAPANESE TEACHERS

Area	Sensei	Kyōin	Rōdōsha	Kenkyūsha	Gakusha
Teacher-pupil relationship	Close, long-lasting, personal; pupil incurs lasting obligation (*on*).	Friendly, less intense, professional. No lasting obligation of pupil.			
Educational goals	*Hitozukuri*, the cultivation of a complete human being. Moral and academic education inseparable.	Academic attainments become a major goal with some attention to moral education in cooperation with the home.		Attention given to learning as a process with interest in how children learn as well as what is taught.	Subject matter and moral behavior both considered as discrete material for transmission.
Teacher's educational responsibility	Unlimited; teacher's inspiration to a moral life most important.	Limited; responsibility for both pupil relationship and professional organization.	Limited	Concern for relevant study and research in subject matter and teaching process.	Must impart his learning to pupils.

TABLE 11 (*Continued*)

Discipline	*Kibishii* (strict and severe); learning is expected to require tough external and self-discipline.	More easy-going; emphasis on group involvement.
Educational exclusiveness	Attendance of pupil is a privilege, not a right. Admitting a pupil is like adopting a son.	All children have a right to education. Teacher should spread efforts equally among pupils.	All children have a right to education.
Teacher	Independent, dedicated, monastic, self-sacrificing.	Organization man, white-collar worker.	Loyal to fellow teachers in opposition to administration.	Pursuit of knowledge, continuing student.	Learned man; knowledge already achieved.

interviews, who stressed that the school should inculcate the sense of obligation (*on*) in the students. He also stressed the goal of "cultivating a human being" in the morals education program of the school. He was strict, severe, and upright in all of his activities observed by the author. At teachers' parties, he drank very little *sake* and maintained a formal demeanor. With students in his classes, he expected deference. He was impatient with stupid answers during recitation and expected his students to learn by rote the assigned subject matter. He encouraged questions, but not discussion.

Mr. Tanaka believed that students should be separated by ability in different schools, as in the prewar system. In all of the behaviors listed in Table 11 under *sensei,* he was in verbal and actual agreement. In each of the areas listed, he falls into the *sensei* rather than the *kyōin* column. But one must add something of both the *gakusha* and *kenkyūsha* roles to completely describe Mr. Tanaka. He was very active in research activities of the school and the community social studies teachers' association. It was he who took the major lead in planning the Nichū experimental morals education program, though he relied a good deal on his reputation for expertise in morals education.

Since he detested the JTU and what it stood for both politically and educationally, he would rate very low on the *rōdōsha* dimension. Thus, the case of Mr. Tanaka shows the way in which the proposed role definitions can be applied to specific individuals, as well as indicating that the *gakusha* and *kenkyūha* roles are not necessarily antithetical.

One older science teacher would rate high on the *kenkyūsha* dimension because of his interest in personal research activities related to his field of scientific specialization, biology. He had a laboratory at home which he proudly displayed to the author, and several technical reports which had been published. At Nichū, he had been responsible for the construction of a very good set of science laboratory materials which were used in the science classes. The science laboratory and supply room was the best-equipped classroom in the school and received very good usage under the direction of this teacher.

Several younger male teachers, active in the youth section of the local union, exemplified the *rōdōsha* role emphasis. One said, in talking about JTU-Ministry of Education conflict, "Since we are all *rōdōsha,* we need a union to protect our livelihood."

A younger female teacher was a staunch supporter of the JTU and its positions on educational issues privately, though she showed no such enthusiasm in public.

In general, the younger teachers could be more closely associated with the *kyōin* and *kenkyūsha* than the *sensei* and *gakusha* role dimensions, but it is important not to carry this generalization very far, for the division of teacher behavior was much more complex.

Two teachers who combined aspects of both the *kyōin* and *sensei* roles were those who carried on their family "weekend and womenfolk" farms while teaching full-time at Nichū. For them, the farmer identification was equally important to the role of teacher. Though they had inclinations toward the strict *sensei* role in their teaching and a belief in the importance of morals education for the "cultivation of human beings," they also were close to the *sarariman* emphasis of the *kyōin* role. They considered their teaching responsibility to be a limited one which they could shed during non-working hours in order to keep up their farm work responsibilities. They did not fit either the *kenkyūsha* or *gakusha* dimensions.

A postscript

THIS CASE STUDY has recorded the selected observations of one Japanese school. It is intended to stimulate an interest in the observation of education in its local environment. It could be called a "rice roots" study, which may reasonably provoke some Japanese scholar to conduct a reciprocal "corn roots" study of a comparable American school.

The report is the result of applying an anthropological viewpoint to the study of a local school. Within this model, the school has been viewed as a community interacting with several other communities, each of which influences the school and is in turn influenced by the school. Following Siegel's suggestion, this view of the school has been called an "acculturation model" (1955).

The model led to specific questions about the school and its relationships with other organizations and groups that have been implicitly asked and partially answered in this report. These questions can be formally stated:

1. What is the social and cultural context of the local school?
2. What are the groups and organizations which significantly affect a local school and its educational programs?
3. What are the goals which these groups and organizations hold for the school?
4. To what extent is there agreement with and commitment to common goals within each group and organization?
5. What is the nature of the interaction of the school and its teachers with these groups and organizations?
6. What are the salient aspects of school organization and activities with respect to explicit and implicit educational goals?
7. What are the ways in which teachers perceive educational goals and conflicts of goals or groups?
8. How do the teachers resolve explicit or implicit conflicts in educational goals?

For an understanding of the social foundations of school education in any specific setting, these questions may be asked and answered. While specifically biased by an anthropological view of human behavior, the questions are suggested to all observers as relevant to the study of educational settings. They are, however, neither sufficient nor complete, in themselves. They should be supplemented by additional studies of individual educational settings in which observers from various behavioral science disciplines will apply their models and viewpoints in cooperative field research.

Each observer brings special competencies to a study, just as each setting has certain unique features. If an anthropologist, an economist, a political scientist, a sociologist, a social psychologist, a social geographer, an historian, a communications specialist, an educator, or another specialist within the behavioral sciences compare notes on observations of the same educational institution, each will perceive and describe a different order of relationships between the school and its setting. The specific questions which they ask and their perceptions of observed human behavior will be conditioned by their disciplinary background. This is as it should be. The important error to avoid in all of these methods of study is the claim that any one discipline or model can give a complete analysis of a particular situation.

In the present study it is important to point out two limitations. First, the analysis has centered on groups and organizations observable in direct contact with the school. Some organizations which have direct influence, but are removed from the school setting, have not been included. The professional schools of education, in which most teachers received their professional education, for instance, have not been described. Second, the questions which other behavioral science disciplines would ask have not been emphasized. The economics, formal politics, and geography of education have intruded only slightly in the descriptions given.

The research methods and analytical outlines of this study were first proposed for their direct relevance to the study of education as an instrument of national policy. These suggestions were directed specifically to the educational planners of developing societies. Without the types of information outlined here, educational planners have little chance of success in efficiently allocating limited educational resources and planning for the contribution which schools can make to their national plans.

Bibliography

ANDERSON, RONALD S., 1959, *Japan: Three Epochs of Modern Education*. U.S. Office of Education Bulletin 1959, No. 11.

BEARDSLEY, RICHARD K., JOHN W. HALL and ROBERT E. WARD, 1959, *Village Japan*. Chicago: University of Chicago Press.

BENEDICT, RUTH, 1946, *The Chrysanthemum and the Sword*. Boston: Houghton Mifflin Co.

CORNELL, JOHN B., "Buraku Social Organization and Community Life," in Bernard S. Silberman (ed.), *Japanese Character and Culture: A Book of Selected Readings*. Tucson: University of Arizona Press, pp. 36–67.

DORE, R. P., 1958, *City Life in Japan: A Study of a Tokyo Ward*. Berkeley, Calif.: University of California Press.

————, 1959, *Land Reform in Japan*. New York: Oxford University Press.

————, 1965, *Education in Tokugawa Japan*. Berkeley, Calif.: University of California Press.

EMBREE, JOHN F., 1939, *Suye Mura: A Japanese Village*. Chicago: University of Chicago Press.

IKE, NOBUTAKA, 1957, *Japanese Politics: An Introductory Survey*, New York: Alfred A. Knopf, Inc.

JAPAN TIMES

KAWAI, KAZUO, 1960, *Japan's American Interlude*. Chicago: University of Chicago Press.

MINISTRY OF EDUCATION, Japan, 1961, *Education in Japan: Graphic Presentation*. Tokyo: Government Printing Bureau (MEJ 6340).

OFFICE OF THE PRIME MINISTER, Japan, 1962, *Japan Statistical Yearbook, 1961*. Tokyo: Japan Statistical Association.

SIEGEL, BERNARD J., 1955, "Models for the Analysis of the Educative Process in American Communities," in G. D. Spindler (ed.), *Education and Anthropology*. Stanford, Calif.: Stanford University Press, pp. 38–49.

SPINDLER, GEORGE D., 1960, *The Transmission of American Culture* (The Burton Lecture, 1957). Cambridge, Mass.: Graduate School of Education of Harvard University.

VOGEL, EZRA F., 1963, *Japan's New Middle Class: The Salary Man and His Family in a Tokyo Suburb*. Berkeley, Calif.: University of California Press.

YANO, TAKASHI, *et al.*, 1961, "Nōson no kenryoku kōzō to kyōiku shokikan no kankei" ("The Power Structure of a Rural Village and its Relation to Various Educational Organizations"), in the *Kyushu University Faculty of Education Bulletin*, No. 8, pp. 135–72.

Recommended reading

ON JAPANESE SOCIETY AND EDUCATION

ANDERSON, RONALD S., 1959, *Japan: Three Epochs of Modern Education.* U.S. Office of Education Bulletin 1959, No. 11.

A short history of modern education in Japan with special emphasis upon the intended reforms of the post World War II American Occupation.

BEARDSLEY, RICHARD K., JOHN W. HALL, and ROBERT E. WARD, 1959, *Village Japan.* Chicago: University of Chicago Press.

A comprehensive case study of contemporary life in a Japanese rural hamlet. Social, cultural, political, economic, religious, and historical facets of community and family life are authoritatively reported.

BENNETT, JOHN W., HERBERT PASSIN, and ROBERT McKNIGHT, 1958, *In Search of Identity: The Japanese Overseas Scholar in America and Japan.* Minneapolis: University of Minnesota Press.

A depth study of cross-cultural educational experience with a brief history of American-educated Japanese students and their later roles in Japanese society and modernization.

DORE, R. P., 1958, *City Life in Japan: A Study of a Tokyo Ward.* Berkeley, Calif.: University of California Press.

A combination of historical analysis and social research report which is the fundamental reference on postwar Japanese urban society.

———, 1959, *Land Reform in Japan.* New York: Oxford University Press.

A social and historical survey of rural Japanese society centering on, but not limited to, the issues and effects of postwar land reform.

———, 1964, "Education: Japan," in R. E. Ward and D. A. Rustow (ed.), *Political Modernization in Japan and Turkey.* Princeton, N.J.: Princeton University Press.

An essay on the ways in which Japanese educational institutions have influenced political institutions during Japan's modern century.

———, 1965, *Education in Tokugawa Japan.* Berkeley: University of California Press.

A sociologist's treatment of educational history which describes the little-known foundation of well-developed, premodern Japanese schools and educational traditions upon which the modern school system is based.

EMBREE, JOHN F., 1939, *Suye Mura: A Japanese Village.* Chicago: University of Chicago Press.

The classic ethnographic report of a prewar Japanese rural village which is important for an understanding of contemporary rural life of such areas as the Uena Region described in this book.

HALL, JOHN W., and RICHARD K. BEARDSLEY, 1965, *Twelve Doors to Japan.* New York: McGraw-Hill Book Company.

An excellent cross-disciplinary introduction to the study of Japan including chapters on geography, history, education, politics, law, and economic development.

KAIGO, TOKIOMI, 1965, *Japanese Education: Its Past and Present.* Tokyo: The Society for International Cultural Relations.

A short history of Japanese education from prehistoric to modern times.

KAWAI, KAZUO, 1960, *Japan's American Interlude.* Chicago: University of Chicago Press.

A lively description of the American Occupation of Japan and the Japanese reaction to American influences of this period. Two chapters are devoted to the American attempts to redirect Japanese education.

MINISTRY OF EDUCATION, Japan, 1964, *Education in Japan: A Graphic Presentation.* Tokyo: Government Printing Bureau (MEJ 6589).

A formal presentation of the current administration and scope of the Japanese school system.

NORBECK, EDWARD, 1966, *Changing Japan.* New York: Holt, Rinehart, and Winston, Inc.

A study which perceptively contrasts urban and rural life in modern Japan through a description of two families.

PASSIN, HERBERT, 1965, *Society and Education in Japan.* New York: Bureau of Publications, Teachers College, Columbia University.

Essays on the development of Japanese education and the modern school system. Historical documents relating to education from the Tokugawa Period to the American Occupation are included.

PLATH, DAVID W., 1964, *The After Hours: Modern Japan and the Searth for Enjoyment.* Berkeley, Calif.: University of California Press.

Report of a recent rural field study in central Japan which concentrates upon the uses of leisure for an understanding of modern Japanese life and society.

SCALAPINO, ROBERT A., and JUNNOSUKE MASUMI, 1962, *Parties and Politics in Contemporary Japan.* Berkeley, Calif.: University of California Press.

A good description of the political process in postwar Japan with a political case study of the events surrounding the ratificaiton of the United States-Japan Security Treaty and the demonstrations which led to the cancellation of Eisenhower's trip to Japan.

SIEGEL, BERNARD J., 1963, "Social Structure, Social Change, and Education in Rural Japan: A Case Study," in G. D. Spindler (ed.), *Education and Culture: Anthropological Approaches.* New York: Holt, Rinehart and Winston, Inc., pp. 530–60.

A short article based upon the field reports of a Japanese anthropologist in two rural hamlets and emphasizing the relations of school and community.

SILBERMAN, BERNARD S. (ed.), 1962, *Japanese Character and Culture: A Book of Selected Readings.* Tucson: University of Arizona Press.
 A well-organized collection of articles on the community, the family, personality development, and national character.

STEINER, KURT, 1965, *Local Government in Japan.* Stanford, Calif.: Stanford University Press.
 A comprehensive and sensitive account of the development and processes of Japanese local government from both a legal and sociological point of view.

TANAZAKI, JUNICHIRO, 1957, *The Makioka Sisters.* New York: Alfred A. Knopf, Inc.
 A novel of Japanese family life in which the interplay of traditional and modern values are expressed in the lives of the characters.

VOGEL, EZRA F., 1963, *Japan's New Middle Class: The Salary Man and His Family in a Tokyo Suburb.* Berkeley: University of California Press.
 An important study concentrating upon the modern Japanese family in an urban setting. Chapter 3 on "The Gateway to Salary: Infernal Entrance Examinations" is very important for an understanding of the social ramifications of the examination system.

ON THE CROSS-CULTURAL STUDY OF EDUCATION

SIEGEL, BERNARD J., 1955, "Models for the Analysis of the Educative Process in American Communities," in G. D. Spindler (ed.), *Education and Anthropology.* Stanford, Calif.: Stanford University Press, pp. 38–49.
 A provocative essay proposing some anthropological models and approaches to the study of education in modern society.

WAX, MURRAY L., ROSALIE H. WAX, and ROBERT V. DUMONT, JR., 1964, *Formal Education in an American Indian Community,* Supplement to *Social Problems* (Spring 1964).
 An important cross-cultural study of education similar in conception to this report of Japanese education, but including recommendations for the improvement of educational practice in the specific setting.

WYLIE, LAURENCE, 1957, *Village in the Vaucluse.* Cambridge, Mass.: Harvard University Press.
 An ethnographic study of a rural French village which provides a balanced report of the relations between school and community as a part of a broader village context.